RECLAIM YOUR POWER

RECLAIM YOUR POWER

Creating Better Mental Health
and Happiness for Life

CRAIG BALL

Copyright © 2021 by Craig Ball

All rights reserved. This book or any portion thereof may not be reproduced or used in any manner whatsoever without the express written permission of the publisher, except for the use of brief quotations in a book review or scholarly journal.

Cover Photo by Andrew Pearson

https://www.andrewpearsonphotography.com.au/

ISBN: 978-0-6453268-0-2

First Printing 2022

Published by Change Seminars 2022

To visit the website and download your handouts from the book, scan below or visit:

https://www.changeseminars.com/reclaim-handouts/

You can reach Craig Ball at info@changeseminars.com, via Facebook at the Men's Mental Health Transformation Facebook group, or to learn more at: www.helpmereclaimmypower.com

DEDICATION

I'd like to dedicate this book, to my wife Theresa
and our 3 beautiful children Harvey, Isla, and Josie.
You are my inspiration and driving force to help others
to live a life as inspiring as the one
you have given me.

CONTENTS

List of Tables and Illustrations..8

About the Author..9

Introduction...11

1. Considerations and Distinctions......................................17
2. Cognitive Distortions or Unhelpful Ways of Thinking 33
3. Basics of REBT 43
4. Unconditional Self Acceptance 58
5. Unconditional Acceptance of Others................................71
6. Affecting your language to facilitate less extremes 82
7. Frustration 93
8. Healthy Negative vs Unhealthy Negative Emotions................ 105
9. Dealing with Shame 124
10. Operationalising your values 139

Further Reading 151

References 152

LIST OF TABLES AND ILLUSTRATIONS

Downloadable versions of all worksheets, tables, and diagrams are available at **www.changeseminars.com/reclaim-handouts** or by scanning the QR code on the copyright page.

Consider clarify and confront matrix – 13

Circles of control – 25, 82

List of Unhelpful Thoughts (Cognitive Distortions) – 42

REBT Tables 47-50, 53-57, 78-79, 99-100, 102-103, 118-120, 127-128, 134, 136-137

Disputation Questions – 64

Self Esteem Equation – 66

Self Esteem Couple – 67

Self Esteem See Saw – 68

Unconditional Self Acceptance OK Illustration – 70

Language Boundaries model – 84

Synonyms for negative emotions table – 90 – 92

Frustration awareness inventory – 96

Healthy Negative Vs Unhealthy Negative Emotions Table – 107- 114

Will Power Model – 141

Core Values List – 145

ABOUT THE AUTHOR

Craig Ball is a former soldier of the Australian Army, professional speaker, and mental health and empowerment mentor. Having served two tours in Afghanistan and dealing with the loss of both mates on the battlefield and through the scourge of suicide post service, he has redoubled his efforts and skillset to focus primarily on men's mental health.

Craig has worked successfully in male-dominated environments delivering this system for over 20 years, his unique experiences and results speak for themselves.

His message is one of hope and that everything you need lies within, sometimes you just need a little guidance to get you moving in the right direction.

Craig holds a degree in psychology, counseling qualifications and is a mental health first aider.

INTRODUCTION

Welcome to Reclaim Your Power, congratulations and thank you for choosing to engage with my system, you won't be sorry, I'm confident of that. If you try and put in the work to make each of the elements of this program part of your habits and system an empowered and happier life awaits. Even improvements in your mental health are highly likely.

Where did it come from?

The system that you have obtained, albeit in a reduced format due to the limitations of a book this size, comes mostly from my study and practice of Rational Emotive Behaviour Therapy (REBT), a type of therapy that can also be considered a philosophy in its own right. Originally it was designed as a philosophy of living but given its effectiveness as therapy was mostly practiced as one and still is today.

Additional elements, hacks, and workarounds that I have added to make my system have come through life experience, using it on myself and the many people that I have had the privilege of working with over the past 20 years or so. It is the reason my own PTSD, Anxiety, and other conditions remain under control and that my life is indeed a pleasant and happy experience.

Whilst I am an optimist, I understand that reality is important to accept and so you will find no strange rah-rah self-improvement techniques used here. Everything contained in these pages is evidence-based. As a final note on the base theory of my system, it was developed by Albert Ellis and was introduced to the world in 1955, is largely based on Stoic philosophy, and originally designed and still practiced today as a 6-week therapy. To the best of my understanding, many in the field of psychology didn't like the idea of only having clients for 6 weeks. So along came someone who is now a very famous psychologist, who took it as his own and watered it down into what is today CBT. As a therapeutic approach, it lasts a lot longer, which pleases the world of psychology, is less confronting which pleases them even more, and certainly from my experience and the feedback from others became less effective.

Some of the key therapeutic elements have also been removed or conveniently forgotten in CBT. I think many of those make REBT more effective some of which we will be using in this book and which I have used with my many clients. Particularly concerning replacing unhealthy negative emotions with healthy negative emotions, but more on this later.

My system has also been honed through my experiences in the Australian Army, at 32 not happy with where my life was going, and having had a few years as a reservist I decided to go all-in and join full time. I was also working hard to develop my business as a professional speaker having had some early success and realised, I needed more life experience to become the speaker and mentor that I wanted to be.

I saw it as being one of two options get into sales, as many speakers have that as a background, or join the army. Afghanistan was also kicking off and I hoped my reserve background which included having passed commando selection a few years prior, would set me up for a deployment to put myself and ultimately this system to the test.

What was to occur certainly gave me that experience and what my system needed to truly be able to add value, to help you through your emotional, psychological upset, difficulties, and ultimately your empowerment and growth. Whilst this book is not a memoir or autobiography by any stretch, it will be peppered with stories from my own experiences throughout and I hope that as this journey continues, we will get to know each other a little better.

Consider, Clarify and Confront

The first of the hacks and workarounds of the base theory of my system comes in the name. I have been developing hacks and workarounds since I first learned about REBT mostly because some of the most important writings by Albert Ellis and others often need simplification.

Academics, as we know, tend to write in complicated ways and this is no different from the writings of REBT. One of my first successes with uncovering meanings and simplifications in this theory came when I was on my primary certificate training in 2003. Before the break, in one lesson, the teacher announced that after the break we would be learning about self-esteem and why it is such a problematic theory and why it holds people back.

At this point, I smiled and the teacher asked, 'Don't you agree with that?' To which I responded, 'No this is the part I have been waiting for.' To that point, I had read 9 books on REBT and still had not been able to decipher one of its most important aspects. You won't have to wait that long and trust me it's a very simple concept to understand.

As the three words in bold above, that you may have read on the cover, indicate there are at a high level only 3 things you have to do in this system. There might be several steps and additional work but at its essence, that's all there is.

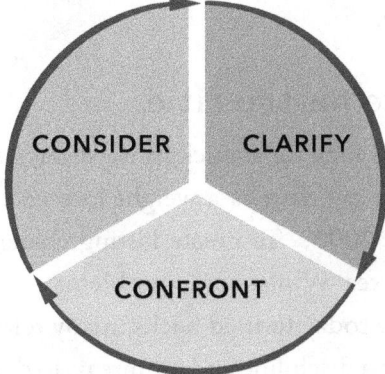

Consider what is happening in your life, what you are currently doing, how you are behaving and, how you will have to start thinking to maximise your outcomes. It's also going to be useful to consider which elements of this system you may already be doing. That's right you are probably already doing many things right or well and this system fits nicely with whatever you are doing that works.

Clarify which beliefs are causing your emotional upset, understanding that we are responsible for our emotional upset. Not blame, but responsibility, which is the other end of a very broad spectrum, accepting this fact can be quite empowering hence the name of the book. How these beliefs manifest is also important as there are typically 4 ways, we each commit the first one and then some combination of the other 3, but more on this later. You will also learn how the beliefs upset you which is vital to clarification however you may already be quite familiar with these.

Confront or challenge your beliefs. This requires questioning your beliefs in several ways, there are 32 of them, give or take but instead we will cover 3 in-depth, which are the three easiest and perhaps most profound. We'll cover off on an additional 3 to give you something else to consider. Confronting your beliefs is one of the areas where the Stoics help us out, as they believed facing up to your problems is key to solving them. It also requires an acceptance of reality and reasoning with ourselves in the way we are intending to start thinking in the future.

Finally, a note on the title.

Whilst everyone is looking for a quick fix these days, something I become very familiar with in my days as a weight loss coach on the FatBlaster product in the early 2000's. To create lasting change and improvement there are no quick fixes. Whilst some problems can be solved with easy solutions or what are today termed hacks, many related issues require us to go deeper, develop a discipline and require us to develop lifelong habits.

People give away their power in a number of ways, by expecting others to do things for them, through lazy habits, or by blaming others for their problems to name just a few. Whilst it may be you who expects others to show up and train them instead of learning to help yourself, or claims that other people have upset you even when claiming such things in an aggressive tone that makes you feel empowered, it's a lie.

You're disempowering yourself. Reclaiming your power is about accepting responsibility, accepting that it's you who chooses how you respond and taking ownership for your life and the outcomes you achieve. That's not to say that when things don't work out it's your fault or to play the blame game as that doesn't help anyone.

It's important to note that the results of reading this book may differ for everyone. Once you feel empowered as a result of using this system and the penny drops it might feel instantaneous and at certain points, you may feel swiftly empowered by new concepts, such as the shame attack exercise later in the program.

Unfortunately, it would be remiss of me not to point out that there are no quick fixes in this life and this book is certainly not one of them. You'll have to do the work and maintain at least some discipline in the application, however, it's typically not much, so at least you have that to look forward to.

So, cheer up, life isn't all that bad after all I have found quick fixes to be only temporary and spurious in nature. The good news is remaining flexible and following the simple model outlined, whilst not a quick fix is not that difficult either.

So read on and enjoy, please share your progress with my system what you have in your hands is essentially my life's work. My gift to you is the gift of rationality because, without it, happiness and all it holds are extremely hard to achieve in any sustainable way.

CHAPTER 1

CONSIDERATIONS AND DISTINCTIONS

> 'Empowerment is never about blame;
> it is about taking personal responsibility'
>
> –BRYANT MCGILL

The chapter titles of this book also follow the names of the modules of my program entitled 'Reclaim Your Power', as of this writing it's a 10 module online mentoring program for men's mental health and empowerment. I believe it's vital to include empowerment as without a self-improvement element any mental health improvement program is only telling half the story. It's leaving out an important opportunity for you and not allowing you to reach your full potential. Without giving people hope and something to aspire to, a better version of themselves, or a better life you are only giving them half a solution and missing a critical opportunity for change.

I want to congratulate you for getting involved, this book is going to take you through a number of different phases and approaches to be able to take care of yourself better emotionally and psychologically. Becoming more effective with your emotions and understanding them, working with them, to be able to clear out a lot of the clutter and bring more of what you want into your life. Unlike some other courses and things, you may have done.

This book is entirely practical. There are skills you can go about using straight away, hence the name Reclaim Your Power. This is an approach that I've used ever since the very early 2000s. It's helped me with several battles throughout my life and I know it will help you with yours. Not only to be okay but to thrive. Like yourself my list is long, I've had to work through bullying, PTSD, depressive disorders, alcohol use disorders, anxiety, and grief. What I will share with you has helped me to not only move forward but to live a much happier, more empowered life.

My outcome for you of the 10 chapters is to learn this new skill and to be able to implement it. To take that leap of faith, to understand, and come on board with what we're doing in this space. To help to reshape your way of thinking so that by the end of it you're able to tackle and work through any of the sorts of issues that come up. In time, to work through them in a way that is almost seamless for you. Whilst this book is no substitute for professional help, something which I actively encourage. It may stop minor problems from becoming bigger ones and help you better articulate what is happening to a therapist should you need one.

It's an exciting time. It's an exciting program to go through just like the online program, however, you'll be reading and not watching videos or participating in zoom calls. I will however be making some of the downloads available. All of the ones that are critical to what we are covering. This is to ensure you get every possible chance to be successful, I've made it possible for the book, like the course to be a participation sport.

The reason I am providing a web page for you to download the various forms for the exercises is that like you I hate it when a book printed like this one in a novel format has stuff for you to fill out in the book. I'd prefer you go to the site, interact with the page and download the activities to complete the work. That way you have the documents that you can re-use again if you wish and a chance to fill them out as if you were doing the course to get a taste, however small, of what it's like to walk with me on this journey.

We are going to cover some distinctions we need to make because it's important that we get our heads in the right space to get the most out of this program, to set you up for success.

It's also vital to understand what we are bringing to the table, what mistakes or errors of thinking are you making? What are you doing well that we need to do more of? What ways of thinking do we need to change?

This is important as many concepts and ideas form part of this program to get yourself across. Some of the main ones early on will not only make the rest easier but will impact you sooner once you become aware of them. This knowledge will allow you to start making changes, whether you realise it or not, at a deeper level.

In this chapter, I will be introducing and discussing some concepts vital to this process that will set you up for the rest of the book. In the second chapter, we will be considering what we bring to the table and learning about and reflecting on what psychologists like to call 'Cognitive Distortions' which sounds like psychobabble to me and most likely you too. Let's just call them thinking errors or unhelpful thought patterns as that's effectively what they are.

Considerations

Firstly, here are a few ways of thinking that form the building blocks of what is covered in this book, an easy way to think about them is that they are assumptions, that once you are aware of them, they will help make what I am going to share with you make sense.

1. Everything is a choice

This pertains to how you got to where you are, what you accept as fair and reasonable, how you view the world, and many other concepts that you probably take for granted. All of these things were to a greater or lesser extent chosen by you. Sometimes it's not a conscious choice, sometimes it was just something you went along with or accepted, guess what? Even those things are a choice.

Here's where it becomes pertinent to this book and my method, the way you look at how your negative emotions are created is a choice. For example, if you're like most people you probably blame others for making you upset when there is another person involved. You may have even blamed them with phrases such as 'stop pissing me off!' when in a rage or one of many other similar phrases.

Perhaps you blame the environment or circumstance when things don't go your way. Many of us do, in fact, it's probably what makes us human. However, there is another way, believe it or not. These responses indicate that we are poor philosophers of our emotional upset and we can choose to look at it in a different way that will help to shape how we feel and our ability to upset ourselves about things. (Ellis, 2019)

That's right we upset ourselves, this is a choice. However, it is a common one so you're not alone. It's often been claimed that human beings are irrational by their very nature but are capable of becoming rational. This is where making a different choice about your emotional upset comes into play. However, for now, just consider that you can make a different choice about your emotional upset and what appears to upset you. We will learn how this occurs in a future chapter.

2. You are not too much of anything

Have you ever been told you are too something? You know that accusation, usually comes in a less than friendly assessment of you by someone. Sometimes someone close to you as a child and then you are left with it. Like a kick in the guts and it can leave you questioning it for years in some cases. I was told that I was too sensitive as a child growing up. This always used to make my mates in the Army laugh. I was called this by my mother of all people, this is a gift and I grew to believe that if you wanted to develop yourself, all you needed to do was determine where you were strong, such as sensitivity and develop complementary skillsets help make this more effective and help bring this gift to the world.

In my case being sensitive helps me to interpret where my audiences are emotionally during a presentation and how to adjust my content and delivery style to best meet their needs. However, I needed to develop coping skills to assist this 'gift' if you like. I recall studying welfare when I first left school and feeling quite sad for people in the stories my classmates, often seasoned welfare professionals would share.

These coping skills could best be described as the difference between sympathy and empathy, and a realization that my feeling sad for them wasn't helping anyone. Least of all me. What have you been accused of being? Is it too angry? I've known plenty of people, many of them in the army, who could have been accused of that. Perhaps they just have a capacity for controlled aggression, something which is considered an asset in certain roles. Being able to turn it on when required for example.

Whatever you have been accused of, this consideration is about calling that label out as bullshit. You are you and we will learn through this program how to handle whatever it is that perhaps is a dominant part of your personality as we go. It's your gift, if you choose to let it be, what you do with that gift is up to you.

3. Strategic Versus Tactical

This way of thinking is important to think about with trying to develop yourself. Tactical is what you do in the moment and strategic is then the planning you do before and after. Sometimes in the heat things don't go to plan and that's ok, just rest assured that it's important to do the planning especially with what I am going to show you. As this will allow you to plan how you are going to think and respond and whilst it might take some work, over time you will begin to get closer to your objective.

You need both ways of thinking to work together, the best example and where I developed a fine appreciation of this was in the military. Tactical is what the troops do on the ground, strategic is what the officers and senior non-commissioned officers do to plan a mission. How this works for improving yourself is setting goals might be strategic, actually completing the steps to achieve them requires the tactical approach, working out ways around setbacks in the moment might form part of the tactics you use.

4. 'Men are not disturbed by things but by the view, they take of them.'

This quote by stoic philosopher Epictetus nearly two thousand years ago is credited with starting an entire movement within psychology, of which the base theory that my system is built around is the foundational version of what today is referred to as CBT. If you are like me and have experienced CBT don't despair, what passes for CBT in most cases is not exactly what I will be sharing with you.

REBT as has already been mentioned is what my system is based on and attempts to remain true to as far as is possible, you will get not only a type of therapy but it is so much more than that. It is a philosophy of living and perfect for not only improving your mental health but also for making you dramatically happier as a result.

Daniel Fryer in the book 'The Four Thoughts That F*ck You Up' mentions how many clients will come for help with a problem, leave six weeks later, and only return a few years later when they have a problem again that they can fix. Ignoring all of what they learned last time, hence why despite the effectiveness of REBT in a therapeutic setting, I believe it is best suited to a self-improvement program such as the one outlined in this book. As you work to make the principles and practice part of your regular habits and practices over time. Making problem-solving and a more supportive philosophy part of who you are.

5. Everything you need is within you

Too much of society today is looking for external solutions and not enough people are interested in looking within. However, if you are prepared to accept responsibility for your happiness, emotional and mental health, the belief that everything you need being within, is an important concept to grasp.

How do I know this? Well, when I reflect upon all of the things that I have been lucky enough to achieve, or anytime I have finished a developmental program or course, the consistent factor for me was, 'I knew I could've already done those things.' Now what I mean by that is often all those courses effectively did was expose me to a part of me I did not already know existed. They manifested those things to me.

They didn't input them, they guided and often supported me to become this new version of who I became. But it was me that became this new version. This is a critical point to consider, the results you can get from my system are you at the end of the day. You will develop and you will become this new and improved version of yourself. But it will be you learning about something new that already resides within.

6. Circles of Concern, Control, and Influence

You may have come across this concept before, but what makes it important is that there is very little you can control and one of the goals of this program is to help you to reduce your circle of concern down to what you can control. At the end of the day, the only things you can control are: What you think, what you feel, what you say, and what you do. Reducing your level of concern down to only what you can control will give you a much greater sense of control and will therefore empower you.

It also greatly assists you, from being swayed by the wind as it were, that every major calamity in the world doesn't get you in such an emotional state that you struggle to function. This is done in many ways in the system and throughout this book as well. By reducing the emotional load and allowing you to function much more efficiently and flexibly in the pursuit of your goals and happiness in general you will be able to achieve more.

It's also a key factor in developing a more optimistic outlook. If we take the quote on optimism from Bram Connolly's book The Commando Way:

'Staying positive does not mean that things will turn out okay, rather it is knowing that you will be okay no matter how things turn out.'

Helping you to be okay by concerning yourself only with what you can control will help make you more resilient and able to remain optimistic no matter what life throws at you. It also requires you to accept the reality of what you can't control and as they say in Alcoholics Anonymous, hopefully, the wisdom to know the difference.

The Serenity Prayer (1934)

God, grant me the serenity to accept the things I cannot change, courage to change the things I can, and wisdom to know the difference.

Fredrich Oetinger (1702-1782) and Reinhold Niebuhr

Circles of Control

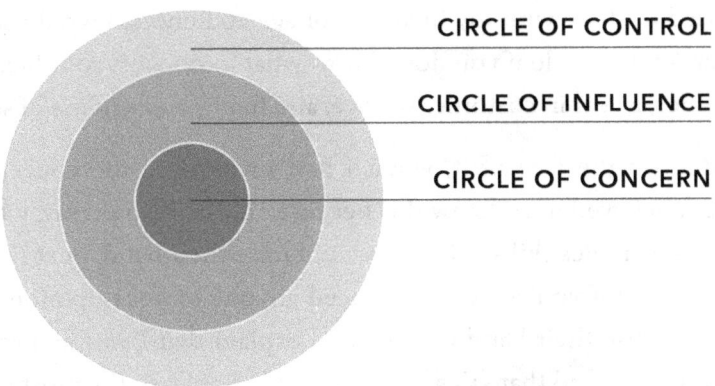

Our circle of influence is something we may never truly know how far it stretches, spending 5 minutes with someone you've never met to explain something, being of service to an organization or community, giving someone hope. This may give them the impetus to be more supportive of others and who knows where that small act of kindness could take them. Influence is substantial. One of the outcomes for my system is that you ultimately increase your circle of influence. Sharing what you read and hopefully practice in this book, will also equip you to help others.

I believe that anyone reading this book isn't just doing it for themselves, you are all altruists in some way shape or form. What you will find throughout this book will give you the skills to do just that.

7. Discipline Equals freedom

I have to give credit where it's due to Jocko Willink for the wording and for reminding me of the power of this Willink & Babin (2018). It's true, however when I think about the most powerful pieces to the puzzle of my development and one of the keys to making my system work, discipline would have to be one of the building blocks.

Back in my 20s when I was trying to determine my life's course, I realised that discipline was key and that I lacked it. I took the path of something I used to share with my high school-age audiences, I would say to them 'here's what to do if you don't know what to do with your life.' Do a year in sales, a year in customer service, and finally a discipline of some sort.'

Often on the face of it, when I first introduced the concept none of them believed me, I knew this because I'd ask. I would say, who believes they need sales skills? No one would raise their hand, next I'd ask: 'raise your hand if you've ever convinced anyone of your opinion.' Everyone would raise their hand to which I'd explain that I was in a room full of salespeople and that sales is, in my opinion at least, the most natural skill we had. I then did the same thing with customer service pointing out the importance of service to others and finally discipline as the glue that held it all together.

Discipline is one of the factors that attracted me to the military, that started with the discipline of getting in shape and maintaining a level of fitness, however, there was so much more. By the time I started to look for work outside my full-time military service the discipline of expecting more of myself was unbelievably high. Certainly, something I could not have developed anywhere else.

If you want to be a disciplined person, it's important to maintain a level of discipline, but like so many theorists on this subject often tell us is that you can have too much discipline. Discipline without flexibility can't work.

However, discipline in my program is required for sticking to the principles and activities, practicing your ABCs, as few as 3 times per week. Simple easy to follow disciplines, being disciplined enough to refuse to rate the self and a few others. All of which will be revealed as we move throughout this book.

8. Forgive yourself

Whilst there are many considerations that you could make, this is the final one that I will list here. In addition to the unhelpful ways of thinking. Perhaps it's the most profound. Forgiveness of self not only liberates you; it leads to tolerance and acceptance of others.

There's a lot more to the considerations as this is just an introduction, as I'm sure you appreciate. What I'm going to be asking you to do now is specify your problems upfront. What you need to do is decide what you want to work on. This particular distinction is vital, as Jim Rohn said it's the difference between being 'a wandering generality vs a meaningful specific'. Please take some time to determine what you are going to work on as we move through this process together.

What are you hoping to work on? What change do you want to see?

Once you've had a bit of time to reflect and consider you will be able to identify what you're going to achieve as part of this.

It's currently a 10-module program. So, what are you going to get out of it? Well you need, and I want you to have a problem to tackle that is occurring in your life. The second thing you need to accept as part of actively participating in the contents of this book is to be coachable. It's one thing for me to say you need to be coachable, but what does that mean?

So, here are the four steps to ensure you are more coachable.

1. Specify your problems upfront
2. Be open to the ABC framework
3. Accept responsibility
4. Share doubts difficulties and blocks to change

These are also agreements that commonly get made between therapists and patients working with REBT, which work well in the coaching and mentoring space.

1. Specify problems upfront

This can also help with what you want to work on, as already alluded to in the next chapter, we are going to look at unhelpful patterns of thought that you may be committing and this will most likely answer this for you. It may also help to ask someone close to you, which ones of these unhelpful thought patterns you are committing as well.

2. Be open to the ABC framework

This point is about being prepared to learn something new. Despite what you may have been taught in other programs and I'm not discounting them at all. They may even complement what we are going to be learning. But despite what you may have been taught I am asking you to take a completely open mind, a sense of wonder if you can and appreciate the ABC process. This is discussed briefly below. We will cover more on this further in the book. Below is a brief outline of the ABC framework.

ABC Model and Keys

- A. Activator
- B. Belief (Key)
- C. Consequences
- D. Dispute (Key)
- E. Enforce Your Preferences (Key)

Activator, this can also be titled adversity or anything that can trigger you. Our problems often arise out of us incorrectly believing that our activators upset us when really, we choose to respond in a certain way. An activator is not a key as we are conscious that we get upset, angry, and stressed out by things, this is the term for those things.

Belief (Key), is a reference for how we feel about the activator. What do I mean by this? Well, it becomes clearer when we get to the next point which is consequence. However, it's your belief about the situation or activator that led to your consequences. This is one of the keys to this process, as it's vital to determining the cause of and solving your problem but it's not always obvious.

Consequence, this is an obvious one that you are familiar with, you get triggered and jump straight to the consequence, often so fast that it looks like the activator caused it. Whilst it's not technically correct as we will learn, it's an easy mistake to make and one that you may be living with right now. Consequence is not a key as you know what they are, although we'll go into much more depth about them soon and you may be living with the consequences of being triggered as you read this.

Dispute (Key), comes into play once we have determined our belief that is causing our upset or consequence. This involves challenging our thinking which can be done in several ways. Which will be discussed in more detail later in the book. Suffice to say you can do a simple disputation of your beliefs by asking the following 3 questions: 1. Is it true? 2. Does it logically follow? and 3. Is it helping?

Enforce Your Preferences (Key), this requires you to accept reality, and further expands or rounds out our disputation. It would usually include saying that of course you'd prefer things weren't the way that they are but unfortunately this is the reality I am faced with and refusing to accept that reality will only make life harder, or words to that effect.

Acceptance of reality can be extremely profound and provide us with a lot of comfort, however, the reality that I am asking you to consider is not the reality of the pessimist but instead that of an optimist. As a lot of my audiences think that being pessimistic, they are somehow wiser, smarter, not to be taken for a fool or something similar.

I advise them that optimists cope better with adversity, have fewer psychological injuries, and live longer. An easy way of looking at optimism, as I mentioned in the section on circles of control, is that optimism doesn't mean everything will be alright, rather it's that despite how things turn out, you will be alright. For a short couple of steps on how to be optimistic and in a way that makes it sound cool too, check out Jocko Willink's 'Good' video on YouTube.

All of the parts of the ABCDE model will be expanded on in the following chapters.

3. Accept Responsibility

Okay, even if you don't do the work, if you try to if you've had a crack, that's all that matters, it's that you are trying, unlike some self-improvement zealots. I don't put much faith in the words of Yoda and say: 'There is no try there is only do' that's BS in my opinion. What I'm asking you to do is accept responsibility for your emotions, which means that to become empowered you need to take back your power, and accepting that you upset yourself gives you back your power. I know it's going to take some work to truly take the leap of faith to realise the benefit of this, but it will come.

What I'm asking you to do is to accept that it's your way of thinking that leads to emotional upset. And what we need to do is have a go at shifting and changing our beliefs around this. That's what accepting responsibility for your erroneous thinking requires working towards becoming rational.

Accepting responsibility is not about blame, the two things are either end of a spectrum. Responsibility empowers you; blame disempowers you. By claiming that you are a terrible individual devoid of any moral worth or similar. Accepting responsibility is about owning the situation and your part in it, you can then move on.

An example of this for me is the psychological diagnosis that I received a few years back. I was diagnosed with PTSD, Generalised Anxiety

Disorder, and some others. It has been my choices to put myself in harm's way that led to me developing these conditions that I fully accept and it is my responsibility to manage them.

By taking the steps for that by calling out situations I find stressful and seeing a counselor regularly allows me to keep it in check

It's not your fault. It is simply your responsibility and just as it's my responsibility to deal with my diagnosis and keep it in check and seek help when required. I commend all of you for being here and for what you've done by picking up this book and getting this far, you are in some way taking responsibility for yourself. Being on this mentoring program, even in this reduced do-it-yourself version via this book, is taking responsibility for your mental health and happiness.

By accepting responsibility, accepting that your actions have either led to the situation or that you accept that circumstances have transpired for the situation you are in to have occurred. It may not always appear like a choice, but what you can choose are your responses to create a different reality.

4. Share doubts, difficulties, and blocks to change.

The next one I want you to consider as we go through is to share doubts and difficulties and blocks to change that you are experiencing. I don't mind if what I am asking you to do flies in the face of something you have done before, that's ok. It is not a problem, talk about it. Just share your blocks. What do you think is blocking you? Have you been exposed to other therapies? Have you done other systems? Write it down.

You might be thinking 'based on the other things I've tried before this is completely different.' That's great. Share that too. Let's have this dialogue. It's vitally important that you get these pieces out and that you're open about it. Much of what I share in this book makes sense to most people so may not be an issue for you, however, it's important to journal out any of these things if they come up for you. If you are doing the online mentoring, you can share those or ask any questions on the regular zoom calls.

It may be something else that you've looked at that is conflicting with that and causing you to doubt or not come on board, blocking you from taking the leap of faith, I get it. That is what I'm trying to get you to do here. Come on board and take that Leap of Faith with me. Once you start to see the results, making the leap of faith makes the next point so much easier which is making a distinction. There are a few distinctions to be made in this program but this is the first, once you get used to it making other clear distinctions, lines that you will no longer cross, become easier as well.

Lastly and most importantly what I want you to do is to start thinking about the biggest problem you're facing right now and how do you want to improve as a result of reading this book? Decide what you want to work on or improve and use that as the focus or a point of reflection as you read through this book and complete any of the exercises throughout.

So that's your responsibility that you need to cover off. Other considerations that are covered in greater detail include overcoming self-esteem but that is a chapter in itself as are the items covered in the chapter on refining our language. However, for now, you have all you need to move to the next chapter which will coincide with much of how you upset yourself moving forward and what you are bringing to your emotional upset in real-time. I highly recommend re-reading this chapter as there are so many things to cover. It will also help you to gain a deeper understanding of this book.

CHAPTER 2

COGNITIVE DISTORTIONS OR UNHELPFUL WAYS OF THINKING

> 'We can't solve our problems using the same kind of thinking we used when we created them'
>
> −ALBERT EINSTEIN

Cognitive distortions as a term sounds like psychobabble. In the interest of keeping things simple, let's just refer to it as what it is, unhelpful patterns of thinking. You'll be familiar with some of these, there are about 15 of them total we, are going to run through them. And then what I want you to do at the end of this chapter is go back and reflect on them and identify the ones that you commit regularly. If you have evolved, and we all do as part of getting older and maturing and feel that you don't commit any of these currently, reflect on what you were once like, behaviours that you once committed. Be honest. A client of mine recently shared that he had committed all of them at some time in his life and he is one of the most well-rounded people I know.

The reason I ask you to reflect and be honest with yourself about these patterns of thinking is whilst you may not have committed them for some time, it's important that you are familiar with how you have tended in the past to behave. The reason for this is that whilst you may have matured and don't act that way much anymore, it's important to remember how you may act given enough stress or a significant setback.

This is because it's likely the way you moved past these behaviours may not have been under pressure. It's a bit like the old saying about fighting or self-defence skills, 'under pressure you don't rise to the occasion you fall to the level of your training'. It's the same with these patterns of thinking that may have been conditioned into you over time. Given the right amount of stress, and it can be very specific, you will fall to the level of your conditioning, or previous behaviours. The other reason I get you to complete the task of identifying your unhelpful patterns of thinking is so that you know what you are up against.

The first cognitive distortion and helpful pattern of thinking we're going to talk about is **Filtering,** which involves focusing on the negative and ignoring the positive. No doubt you've met these sorts of people, you may have been one. They love to just constantly share their negative mood or negative mindset. Hopefully, you had a chance to watch Jocko's video; Good, if not get on YouTube and check it out it only takes a couple of minutes and is a really good circuit breaker for this type of behaviour.

Essentially what he says is that if you're capable of saying good irrespective of how negative things feel you should be able to pull yourself out of the situation that you have allowed yourself to wind up in. It reminds you how to find the good, to navigate your internal politics on a deeper level by rallying you to not only say but believe in the single syllable word. I've used this video with some heavy blue-collar male audiences who looked at me with skeptical eyes when I dared to suggest being optimistic. You know that look, you've probably had it yourself. That belief is that you are somehow wiser by being this way. After showing them that video, they were saying good every chance they got throughout the workshop and by the end of it, they were bouncing off the walls and excited. The next time I presented to them their boss said 'I was waiting for the good video again'.

So, all these things occur nothing happens overnight but being aware of these unhelpful patterns of thinking is a great way to get started towards improving yourself. **Polarised Thinking** is another really good one. It's also known as dichotomous thinking which is all or nothing thinking, ignoring the complexity. Something's either good or it sucks.

As I've mentioned already, life isn't black and white. In life, as we know, there are many shades of grey and we have to learn to work through and live in those shades of grey to give us some sort of flexibility.

We discuss a little later in the book about bringing your tools, in doing this you are getting a little bit better at tailoring your approach to this way of thinking that REBT asks of us. This philosophy and getting away from all-or-nothing thinking, leads to less catastrophizing, by acknowledging the complexity of life, helping you to think more flexibly.

Control Fallacies assumes only self or others are to blame. Always looking for someone to blame or beating yourself up. We all know people like that, the ones that assume themselves always to blame may not be that obvious. However, I am currently working with a client who has blamed themselves for more than 12 years for not speaking up when they 'should have' leading to a catastrophic event. It's a great way to be your worst enemy.

The Fallacy of Fairness assumes life should be fair and this often happens when we get quite upset with things, things according to this unhelpful pattern of thinking that should be fair. It fits into one of the original irrational beliefs that we're going to talk about in an upcoming chapter, irrational beliefs about self, others, and circumstance. When things appear to be on top of us and it appears not to be because of another person or our performances but because of the circumstances.

The circumstance should be fair, consider it in the context of your driving to a job interview in your best suit and making good time then you hit a traffic jam or get a flat tyre or both. If the circumstance triggers you to want to get out of the car look up at the sky and declare 'Why Me God? Why Now?' Or something similar you may be stricken by the fallacy of fairness.

Unfortunately, life isn't fair, and having a reality-based perspective helps us to realize and understand that, so it's about awareness as much as anything else.

Overgeneralization is next. This doozy of a thought pattern tends to assume a rule from one experience. Overgeneralisation can also occur between yourself, your successes, and your failures, which we discuss further in the chapter on unconditional self-acceptance or USA. Many people assume rules about all kinds of crazy stuff. Some even assume rules about an experience they didn't even have, someone, told them something and off they go.

Emotional Reasoning is one of the other really interesting ones. And this is why I encourage you all to continually challenge yourself because it states that 'If I feel it, it must be true'. Remember you are the easiest person in your life to convince of anything and by convince it can also mean fool yourself of anything. So, get away from the emotional reasoning, realize just because you feel something to be true does not necessarily mean that it is. This is different from intuition, but it may sometimes masquerade as intuition. For examples of the difference, I highly recommend the book 'The Gift of Fear' By Gavin de Becker. This and other books mentioned throughout are listed in further reading or the reference list at the end of the book.

The Fallacy of change is the next one. This is a great one, this old chestnut expects others to change, now this is easy for me to say being a change manager in my consulting life. It's about helping people to deal with changes being made in the workplace and helping them to adapt and sometimes cope. Many people won't change, that's why it's such a difficult job for some, I've given up expecting others to change years ago. I do believe you have to be the change you wish to see in the world. I was even encouraged by someone I respect years ago to discover my why. Not as wishy-washy a term as it may first appear and the benefits have been great. My why is 'To leave the world in a better place than how I found it.' It's ok if it doesn't resonate with you, it's not supposed to, but it does indicate a degree of change for the better. But none of these things include expecting others to change, whilst I stay the same. I mean that drags us if taken far enough, into the world of the narcissist and nobody wants to go there.

Shoulds are another great one, this requires one to hold tight to personal rules of behavior to judge self and others if those rules are broken. Judging yourself and others if those rules are broken is a great way to drive yourself nuts, especially if people don't know or appreciate what those rules are. There's a term in REBT or commonly used phrase about the behaviour of shoulds. People committing this one end up shoulding all over themselves.

Things are going to be the way they're going to be concerning others' behaviour, you may be able to influence it slightly, but unless people sign up to a charter of behaviour or code of conduct, which is unlikely, no one is going to follow your rules. Expecting others to live by the rules you set for yourself is a great way to piss yourself off. Rigidly holding onto those rules for yourself can tie you up in knots also, remaining flexible whilst not a chapter, is a constant theme in this book and system.

I've often asked successful people when I meet them, do you judge others by the standard you set for yourself? That's a shouldism right there.

Catastrophising expecting the worst-case scenario and minimizing the positive. This, as we will discuss in the chapter on irrational beliefs and how they manifest, is one of the 4 main ways that they occur. Claiming that a difficulty you may be experiencing is 100% bad, awful and it couldn't get any worse. When this occurs it is untrue, as the old saying goes 'from the day you are born till you leave in a hearse, something isn't so bad that it couldn't get worse.' But no doubt you or someone you know has got some experience with this one.

Catastrophisers can also be just your everyday pessimist, always expecting things not to work out and claiming that it's nice when things do. They are pleasantly surprised, but they often feel crap the rest of the time. Honestly, why do it to yourself, as I have told people I know like this, being an optimist means I don't need to play these silly games with myself and I'll be able to cope better with adversity. If you are making a conscious choice as this book and my program advises, choose optimism. Remember being optimistic doesn't mean thinking things will always work out, that's delusional, it's knowing that regardless of how things turn out you'll be ok. This can be achieved once you harness the power to reduce your circle of concern down to your circle of control.

Less catastrophising is one of the outcomes of optimism and reducing our circles of concern to what we can control. So too is reducing our language to less extremes, which we cover in a later chapter.

Heaven's reward fallacy is the next one, those people who expect their self sacrifice to be rewarded. You might get a lot of these people on volunteer committees. If you're one of those people who self-sacrifice you feel as if you're wearing a badge of honor because you're feeling the pain of others or that you're putting in for them. This can occur in several ways, often overly sympathetic people can be like this. I usually ask them does it feel more real if you're feeling this way, you feel as if you need to do that. It can become tiresome and wear you out. It's not unlike the Shoulds, as after a while you might feel that people should acknowledge your efforts. These sorts of people tend to get noses significantly out of joint when they don't get rewarded or acknowledged for that. The fallout for them tends to manifest as life is not fair.

Always being right, this one is probably one of the most unlikeable human behaviours and often makes me wonder if the people who behave this way get tired of themselves. It can also manifest in a number of similar ways. People who always have a better story than yours, regardless of whether there is a story, to begin with. I once worked in an office and the PR guy always had a better story. One day I was assisting with a trial of a product and had people in my network volunteer to try the product and give feedback. It wasn't a double-blind placebo trial, with strict guidelines or anything like that, but it was important at the time to test the efficacy of the product.

One of my mates lived not far from the office so I dropped some samples off for him, he had a case of red wine at the house and gave me a bottle. Later that day at the office, the bottle of wine was sitting on my desk, and along comes the PR guy, the first words out of his mouth were, 'when I worked at XYZ bottle shop we had much better wine than that!' To which I replied 'You Win! Congratulations by this stage I was tired of this as you could well imagine, no doubt you have suffered similar types of people.

The flip side of this behaviour and equally annoying is people who are never wrong, they scapegoat, they give excuses, but wrong? Never! It's like some kind of game for them. When accepting responsibility, the never wrongs can be quite difficult. They fear it, assuming it will lead to blame, creating their problems is a well-honed skill for some of them.

At least these days they are teaching kids not to fall victim to this habit, for those of you familiar with the Australian cartoon Bluey about a family of sheepdogs. In the episode in question, Bluey the main character has an argument with Bingo her younger sister that their grandparents, two older cattle dogs in retirement accommodation, can't be taught the dance move flossing. This is attempted on an iPad.

Once the poor old confused grandparents get it wrong enough times and bingo walks off frustrated, a victorious Bluey rubs Bingo's nose in it, then wonders why Bingo is upset and won't play with her. When Bingo shares this with her mother, a red cattle dog, she asks 'is it more important to be right or is it more important to have someone to play with?' Bluey then goes and patiently teaches the grandparents to floss, proving Bingo right. That might be a good question to ask someone, or yourself if you are prone to this one.

Personalisation, always assuming self responsible/blaming the self, often with little, or no evidence. Taking everything personally as if they were to blame for their friends having a bad time or more severely believing that you are responsible for every bad mood or upset of those around you.

It's very ego-driven and inaccurate in that it would be quite an achievement if you could affect that many people, it also discounts that they have their thoughts and lives to be so focused on, that they are interested enough to let you upset everyone's mood. A little introspection might help to realise that this may not be the case. Once again important to be aware of if this is you.

Jumping to Conclusions, or fortune-telling, this pattern thinking requires the perpetrator to make conclusions and predictions based on little or no evidence and believe them to be the gospel truth.

Global Labelling, is an extreme version of overgeneralisation and is common practice in the habit of self-esteem. One of the problems with it is that it doesn't stop. It's a habit, you overgeneralise about something positive that feels good, you do something well and get some recognition for it. Someone refers to you as a legend, you might fist pump the air, even say to yourself 'legend'. Then what do you call yourself when things don't work out, overgeneralisations about being an idiot or a failure soon follow.

A simple method I use to remind myself and hopefully others of the folly of overgeneralisation is to name the habit as something you might call someone who does whatever it is. Someone who jumps to conclusions is a conclusion jumper, which sounds silly but so is the idea of overgeneralising. You might like to have a go if you commit this one or know someone who does.

Blaming, assuming everyone else is at fault. This one follows from always being right. We tend to commit this one when we erroneously assume that someone else pissed us off. Possibly one of the most common unhelpful patterns of thinking. It indicates that we are poor philosophers of our problems, 'That Jerk cut me off!' or any situation really where there is a belief about the other person's involvement 'causing' our emotional upset.

We will discuss this one at length in an upcoming chapter on the basics of REBT when discussing revealing to ourselves or to help others to determine the belief that is at stake at the center of our upset. Often the recipient of our blame has no knowledge of or at the very least had no intention of influencing our emotional upset in this way. Despite this, they are most likely oblivious to it anyway. What a great thing to hold onto.

So, to recap on the unhelpful ways of thinking, so that you can circle which ones you resonate with and which ones you need to work on or discard, here they are again.

Unhelpful Thoughts (Cognitive Distortions)

1. Filtering	9. Catastrophising
2. Polarised Thinking	10. Heavens Reward Fallacy
3. Control Fallacies	11. Always Being Right
4. Fallacy of Fairness	12. Personalisation
5. Overgeneralisation	13. Jumping to Conclusions
6. Emotional Reasoning	14. Global Labelling
7. Fallacy of Change	15. Blaming
8. Shoulds	

CHAPTER 3

BASICS OF REBT

> 'Men are disturbed, not by things but by the view which they take of them'
>
> —EPICTETUS

In this chapter, we are going to work through how to find clarity in your emotional and psychological upset, so if you can recall what problem you were going to work on as part of reading this book, now would be a good time to recall what that was. If not, come up with something that you would like to work on in this chapter.

As we will be effectively learning to coach ourselves in this and the next chapter it's important that we reflect on a few things covered so far so that you get the best outcome. This means we have to remember our four points to make us more coachable, they were:

1. Specify your problems upfront
2. Be open to the ABC framework
3. Accept responsibility
4. Share doubts difficulties and blocks to change

In this chapter, we need to start with a problem as indicated above. That can be something as simple as a situation where you experienced a level of stress, anger, frustration, or other unhealthy negative emotions (there is a difference between, unhealthy and healthy negative emotions which we will discuss later) that reached an intensity level of 7 out of 10 or greater.

Be open to the ABC framework as we are going to learn what that is in greater detail and how that fits together. Simple yet surprisingly complex, believe it or not. To get the most out of what we are about to cover, you'll need to accept emotional responsibility. That is accepting that you choose to respond a particular way, I know it may feel like you don't choose, or that it occurs so quickly that taking the time to choose is not possible, but it is and if you accept that it might be it will help us go through this.

The easiest way to grasp that one, is from a lesson I learned as a kid in my second year of school. I had a teacher whose name was Mrs. Van Egla, not sure if that is the correct spelling but she was a very matter-of-fact lady. One day she said to us, humans are not like dogs in one very important respect. No, it's not defecating in public, she didn't say that I'm just trying to lighten the mood as she was also a very serious person. Her analogy was that if you accidentally step on a dog's tail it will react automatically to defend itself, it might bark at you or swing around and bite you or something similar. Human beings can stop and consider our response. I like to refer to this part of our makeup as the space to consider a more rational response.

Accepting emotional responsibility is about finding that space and making a habit of using it. Mrs. Van Egla, didn't explain it quite like that, I mean come on I was only 6 and the wisdom stopped at we don't react automatically like dogs but that explanation has stayed with me all this time.

Finally, before we get our feet dirty in the ABCDE model and how it works, sharing your doubts, difficulties, and blocks to change, might not be that easy from a book. So please if you haven't already, go to my Facebook group, the Men's Mental Health Transformation, join and share it there. Tag me in the post and I will respond, it's also important to share it as others will learn from it, as they may have felt the same way.

If you remember there were five elements of REBT, the ABC model if that's not enough letters of the alphabet for you, there are 2 more D and E. So how does this work?

Your Beliefs the B of the ABCDE model, are the part of you that is triggered by an Activator, or Adversity which is the A in the model that you don't quite realize and you'll learn as we go through the activities exactly how that occurs in the great period of self-discovery in this chapter and the next. I think you're going to come out the other side of it with a fantastic new perspective.

We'll look at the Consequences or part C of the model that these activators lead to and it is both the activators and consequences that are not considered the keys of this model by my definition because you are already aware of them. You experience them every day. You know that you get triggered, you know that you react, what happens in between and the way that you deal with them are the keys. You are now going to learn how to respond and act consistently with the three keys.

As we go through this model, we will reference many of the unhelpful patterns of thinking that you read about in the last chapter, how we address them will help to make my model of Consider, Clarify and Confront approach make more sense as well. There's a lot to go through from such a simple concept.

To begin following the ABCDE model as close to that order as possible, requires a discussion of a concept that once again sounds like psychobabble, thanks again psychology. The concept is called psychological interactionism, and I'm not making that up. So, what occurs as you will have seen in the earlier chapters is:

A. Your get triggered by an Activator or some form of adversity

B. We'll come back to B in a minute as I want to first cover off on what you already know and how you experience it. I did say we'd follow it as closely as possible but that means not necessarily in a linear fashion.

C. You experience the effects of being triggered, although for many of you it might not be interpreted as being triggered although that is more accurate. Your Consequence or C at this point comes in 3 types, Thinking, Feeling, and Behaving. Thinking and feeling logically follow from one another because you think as you feel so it's often claimed that consequences come in two ways.

So, you feel something and you do something, it appears as if the Activator made you do it, at least that's the common interpretation. The reality is you were triggered or at least your rational preference was triggered.

We all have rational preferences, most of us prefer to be respected. Some people pay a lot of money not to be respected but this book isn't about that subject. Most of us prefer that our efforts achieve at least something close to the outcome we hoped and most people prefer that circumstances work in our favour.

The problem arises when our preferences get triggered, and shoot up rather quickly, in fact so fast you can't tell, to become irrational or must beliefs.

> B. beliefs are what becomes of your rational preferences when triggered, they come in three types, a bit like your preferences.
> They are beliefs about self, others or the circumstances.

The way you determine which belief is fairly simple, in fact, it's probably the easiest part of my whole program. It's perhaps easiest explained if I attempt to make a basic diagram as I explain it.

A. Activator: Identify your activator or trigger	B. Belief: Circle all that apply Self Others Circumstance	C. Consequence: Identify your feelings and how you behave when triggered by this activator
Next ask yourself in a sentence, I get triggered by_____ I feel _____ and behave in an _____ manner **BECAUSE OF WHAT?**		

Note that I put the big complicated question in capitals, that's all it is 'because of what?' Document your responses if doing this activity by yourself. Usually, your first few sentences will indicate fairly clearly what belief you are dealing with. It may be the case that you have a combination of one or more and sometimes all 3 happening at once. In that situation, it's important to acknowledge all of them and decide which is more intense than the others and work on that first.

So, sit back and review what you have said or written and decide, have you blamed someone? If so, it might be about others, have you blamed yourself? Is it just dumb luck? Was it dependent on the weather? That would indicate that it is about the circumstance.

Once you have determined which beliefs you have to work out it's important to understand how they manifest. Most REBT texts discuss this, however, the best book I have discovered on this subject in recent years is called The Four Thoughts that F*ck you up. That's actually how it's written on the cover. The Author is Daniel Fryer a psychotherapist from the UK, if you join the Facebook group mentioned earlier, Men's Mental Health Transformation, in the announcement section you can watch an interview of him.

What I liked most of all was how easy to understand and implement his advice on how beliefs manifest for us. Effectively the four thoughts are the four ways beliefs manifest, they are:

1. Demandingness
2. Catastrophisation
3. I can't standitness
4. Pejorative putdowns

The majority of us commit demandingness in most situations, and can and often do commit one of a combination of the other three. Demandingness implies that you demand that things be other than they are. Which is often linked to a failure to accept reality. Acceptance of reality is a big deal with emotional upset and quite common, refusing to accept reality can impact our emotional wellbeing to a fairly high degree.

Catastrophisation as we have already discussed in the considerations section involves the belief that something is 100% bad awful, and horrible and couldn't possibly get any worse under any circumstances. Of course, we know this to be untrue but just like failing to accept reality, this is, quite a big deal for people. I can't standitness is not a real word, also described as I can't standititis, and I can't copes as Daniel Fryer has termed it.

Pejorative putdowns or the as the name suggests implies that someone else or yourself is to blame as a result. This can also extend to circumstances, statements such as life sucks, the world is useless and terms similar to that.

So, if we return to our table from before, you might like to follow along and draw your own table to cover all of the points. The table is available for download at **www.changeseminars.com/reclaim-handouts**

A. Activator: Identify your activator or trigger	B. Belief: (Circle all that apply) Self Others Circumstances	C. Consequence: Identify your feelings and how you behave when triggered by this activator

> Next ask yourself in a sentence, I get triggered by _____ I feel _____ and behave in an _____ manner **BECAUSE OF WHAT?**
>
> **My Belief manifests as:** (Circle all that apply):
> 1. Demanding
> 2. Catastrophising
> 3. I can't standititis
> 4. Pejorative putdowns

If you are creating your table at home just add the beliefs and the ways that they are manifesting for you. I have created the table this way to cover all of the options. So, to give you an example to start you off and one that is common to many.

A. Activator: Identify your activator or trigger	B. Belief: (Circle all that apply)	C. Consequence: Identify your feelings and how you behave when triggered by this activator
Getting cut off in traffic	Self (Others) (Circumstances)	**Feelings:** Anger, frustration **Behaviour:** Yell and scream, hit the horn, flash your heads lights, drive up behind them. Close the gap to stop them from getting in

> Next, ask yourself in a sentence, I get triggered by getting cut off in traffic I feel angry and frustrated and behave in an abusive manner **BECAUSE OF WHAT?** They shouldn't drive recklessly; people don't respect one another anymore. I feel unsafe, how dare they almost drive into me, this person is an idiot!

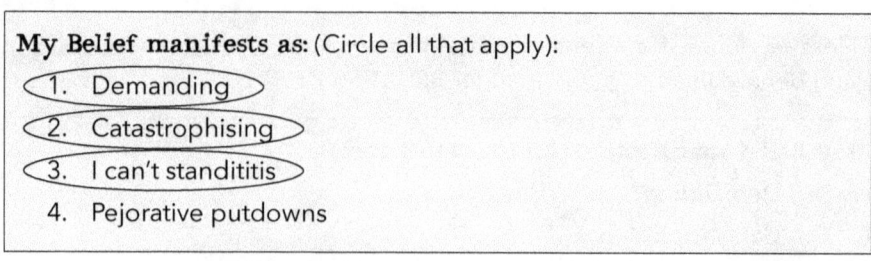

So, the main thing that I want you to take away at this point is how this process allows you to clarify what is happening for you. It's a functional approach as it takes what you are saying, how you are explaining it to yourself, your self talk and puts the pieces into the model to help you to see what has occurred.

The next step in the process is to confront what we are thinking, challenge ourselves, and here is where we start to build resilience into our way of thinking. By facing a challenge with a challenge, to take on the adversity and what is triggering us in a way that leads us to think more flexibly. In doing so it allows us to adapt to the situation more.

As we start to challenge our thinking you can remove the negative energy out of how we are feeling, this is where the third option for dealing with our problems comes in. As men in western society and for women too, we are taught growing up there are two options for dealing with a stressful situation or emotional upset.

Option 1. is to yell and scream about it, to hit something, to get in the person's face about it, or to by any other definition 'rage out' about the problem. To get angry pissed off, and refuse to take that crap. This approach on the surface appears to give you back your power and is certainly a good example of emotional reasoning. You might recall in our unhelpful patterns of thinking, emotional reasoning states: if I feel it, it must be true. This is why Option 1. is so popular.

The problem with Option 1. is that whilst it gives an erroneous feeling of control, all it does is reward that behaviour, and over time it can start to become an almost automatic response. This then can make the perpetrator of Option 1. feel that they are almost being controlled by that response. Listening to loud music is probably a fairly healthy way to commit Option 1. and not to claim hitting something necessarily is a bad thing, as exercise can be a very effective way to deal with the stress of negative energy arising from emotional upset. If boxing or boxercise is your thing go for it!

Option 2. is to bottle up your problem, to not get angry, to just go along. To 'deal' with it as people often say. To suck it up even, this can come out in other ways. Transference can occur as a result of bottling up your problems, you can apportion blame and anger to someone or a situation other than the one that has caused you problems. An indication of this may be feelings of anger in situations that might not normally warrant that behaviour from how you would normally act.

An example of this from parenting for me is when playing with my son Harvey, at one stage when he got excited or at other random times, he would punch me in the groin. I'm sure many parents have gone through this at some stage. The problem for me that I explained to him, whilst I would often respond angrily if I was hit hard enough, is that the anger from this incident would influence my treatment of him if he was naughty later in the day. I would transfer that negative energy to another incident of bad behaviour. Leading me to come off as angry for most of the day.

This brings us to Option 3. which we are never taught and which we may never discover and if we do, we may never attribute it to the solving of our problems. Once you practice this and make it part of your regular way of thinking or your philosophy, it can make life easier than you ever thought possible and over time occur in many cases almost automatically.

Option 3. involves disputing our beliefs and the statements we make about them, to challenge them. A simple way almost like the quick start guide version to challenge your problems is to ask:

1. Is it true?
2. Does it logically follow?
3. Is it helping?

Is it true, requires you to examine evidence of what occurs and also to consider what you may not know about the situation. How the other person may be feeling and what they may have had happen for them at the time are also worth considering with this question. It also alludes to the fact that much of our emotional upset involves making inferences about a situation and responding to those inferences without bothering to see if they are true.

In using, is it true? to challenge your way of thinking, you can also bring in unknowns such as did that person intend to upset you? Have they simply made a mistake? Don't we all make mistakes from time to time?

Does it logically follow? This question addresses the concern about force escalation or appropriateness of the response. This is a term from my time as a security guard and as a soldier. Force escalation in the military and security came down to whether the use of force was excessive and therefore fair. An appropriate response to an aggressive person might have been to engage with them verbally lowering your voice or energy level apologizing that they feel that way and making them feel heard to attempt to solve the problem.

This is to engage in or attempt to de-escalate the force being used and bring some rationality to the situation. Inappropriate use of force would be to use a weapon or attempt to hit the person if they had not thrown a punch for example or began posturing physically. Shooting someone at a checkpoint who is unarmed and has not indicated any weapons are on their person is another example of this.

Therefore, if someone cuts you off, and that leads you to be stressed at a level equal to or greater than seven out of ten, you follow them for the next 200 kilometers when they get out you run and bash their window in, that's excessive, that is over the top. I'm sure you'll agree. That's when it's getting to a problem, or even if you follow them for the next ten kilometres, then try to scare them.

The question, does it logically follow that you do any of these things? helps us to stop and say perhaps not. It encourages us to think just a bit about how far we are taking things. If you are not beginning to waver in your conviction of just how hard you are holding on to your stinking thinking then the final question; is it helping? really should help you to stop in your tracks and take stock.

Continuing with our table:

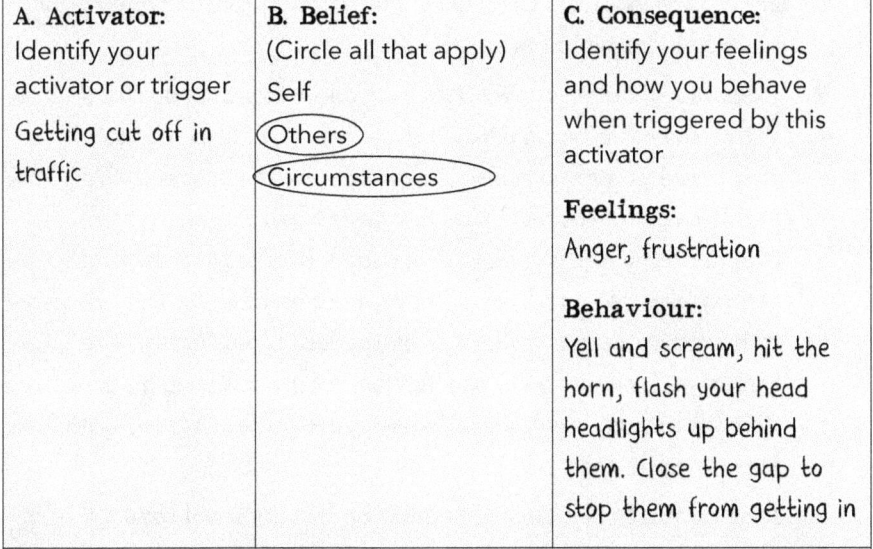

A. Activator: Identify your activator or trigger	B. Belief: (Circle all that apply)	C. Consequence: Identify your feelings and how you behave when triggered by this activator
Getting cut off in traffic	Self ⟨Others⟩ ⟨Circumstances⟩	**Feelings:** Anger, frustration **Behaviour:** Yell and scream, hit the horn, flash your head headlights up behind them. Close the gap to stop them from getting in

Next ask yourself in a sentence, **I get triggered by:** getting cut off in traffic I feel angry and frustrated **and behave** in an abusive manner **BECAUSE OF WHAT?** They shouldn't drive in a reckless way; people don't respect one another anymore. I feel unsafe, how dare they almost drive into me, this person is obviously an idiot!

My B manifests as: (Circle all that apply):
1. **Demanding** ⭕
2. Catastrophising
3. **I can't standititis** ⭕
4. **Pejorative Putdowns** ⭕

D. **Dispute:**

1. **Is it true?** Is it true that when I get cut off in traffic, the person who cut me off is a complete idiot? No, it's not, they perhaps didn't see my car and forgot to check their rear vision properly. They may have been in a rush with a lot on their mind. In truth I don't really know what is going on for them and getting angry and declaring their status as an idiot, is not only unfair but also likely hard to prove and an example of jumping to conclusions.

2. **Does it logically follow?** Does it logically follow that, because this person has driven in a way that could be considered reckless that I need to respond in a reckless manner towards them? Is this a recklessness competition? Does it logically follow that this person is disrespecting me? Well other than putting their car in a dangerous position that I need to drive differently to compensate for and indicate to them that there is another car on the road by flashing lights or honking my horn (not both) and hopefully not by locking up my brakes although this may be required. I do not need to follow and intimidate them to get revenge.

3. **Is it helping?** Is it helping the situation that I yell and scream, attempt to punch a hole in my steering column, though it may be the case that I would have to be superman to achieve this, the answer is most likely no. Is it helping that I feel the urge to intimidate them to get revenge with my car or worse? No, as it's time-consuming and an energy drain, dangerous and I could get myself arrested or worse.

> **E. Enforce your preferences:** Of course, I'd prefer that people didn't cut me off in traffic and lead me to believe that they are somehow attempting on purpose to disrespect me. But they do and as long as I can choose to respond in better more helpful ways to this situation, I can deal with it effectively.
>
> Whilst I'd prefer people didn't cut me off in traffic, it happens, and whilst ever I drive, the reality is that it could and does happen and I'd better get used to it as it makes as much sense as being pissed off by the rain.

Let's look at a different situation that might be stressful for you and walk through the ABCDE model as we go.

Most people hate public speaking. It's only a few rare ones like myself, that actually really like it. You get asked to present to a group, most people would rather do just about anything else. Even being asked to present could trigger someone, especially when it's someone like your boss.

Activator – being asked to speak in front of a group of people,

Consequence – your first response might be 'How dare that person ask me to speak. I can't say no.' This self-talk might result in you feeling anger, fear, and nervousness. You might behave by experiencing a physiological feeling of fear, you might avoid them, stutter in your response and get sweaty palms.

'It's my boss, what am I going to do?'

When you ask the question: When I get asked to present in public to a group of people, by my boss, I feel Nervous and get sweaty palms, start to panic because I don't want to do a bad job, I feel pressured, I hate presenting, my boss is being unfair. Why can't your boss ask this?

These responses indicate that the beliefs are mostly about yourself and might also be about your boss, but for the most part, they are beliefs about yourself.

Putting this problem into our table will help us to have more clarity around it.

A. Activator: Identify your activator or trigger Being asked to present to a group of people in public	B. Belief: (Circle all that apply) (Self) (Others) (Circumstances)	C. Consequence: Identify your feelings and how you behave when triggered by this activator **Feelings:** Nervous, anxious **Behaviour:** Dry mouth, start to stutter in reply, sweaty palms

Next, ask yourself in a sentence, I get triggered by getting asked to speak in public and I can't get out of it. I feel anxious and nervous and behave fearfully **BECAUSE OF WHAT?** I hate public speaking, am not very good at it. I just know I'm going to look like an idiot what if I get it wrong? How could my boss be so unfair and ask me?

My Belief manifests as: (Circle all that apply):

1. (Demanding)
2. (Catastrophising)
3. (I can't standititis)
4. (Pejorative Putdowns)

D. Dispute:

1. **Is it true?** That, I will look stupid when I present, hardly I'm not a professional presenter and I am simply going to do my best. Is it true that my boss is being unfair? No, my boss needed someone to share the work that my team has done on this project and I am best placed to share the information due to my role.

> 2. **Does it logically follow?** That I need to get anxious and stutter and think that I will look like an idiot and claim that it is 100% bad? No, it does not, I speak to people all day and it's the same thing only standing up.
> 3. **Is it helping?** Is it helping that I respond this way? No, it's not, ruminating over my fear and constantly imagining the worst-case scenario, which is all in my head only seeks to detract from the good job I believe I can do.

> **E. Enforce your preferences:**
>
> Of course, I prefer that my boss didn't put me on the spot and ask that I deliver a presentation. Of course, I'd prefer that I not look like an idiot. Unfortunately, by the nature of my work sooner or later I am going to be asked to present. Most people find it difficult and that's ok

A copy of the above form, including the above examples and a version of our table with blank spaces for you to fill out, is available at: **www.changeseminars.com/reclaim-handouts** or by scanning the QR code at the start of the book.

You might have noticed in the D. Disputation and E. Enforce your preferences section in both examples that I appear or have attempted to make the assumptions about the trigger to appear silly or to use humour. That's the point. Humour is one of the most important parts of helping you to move beyond your irrational beliefs and to feel happier and more emotionally healthy.

Despite not being as aggression-based in terms of the response it can illicit, being asked to speak in public could easily manifest all of the irrational beliefs at B and those beliefs could manifest through all of the 4 ways. It's often been said that public speaking is the number one fear of all people, they fear it more than death. As a former mentor of mine Doug Malouf used to say 'that means at a funeral most people would rather be in the box than giving the eulogy.'

CHAPTER 4

UNCONDITIONAL SELF ACCEPTANCE

> 'Self Esteem is the greatest sickness known to man or woman because it's conditional.'
>
> —ALBERT ELLIS

I'm so glad you made it this far. This is where we get into some deeper elements. We've worked through some important points of the ABC model, but there is a lot more to REBT and how it can go about shaping your way of thinking and your life at its core. By this I mean, your philosophy, the way you do what you do.

I'm referring to what has been touted as the most liberating concept in all of self-improvement and unless you know where to look it may pass you by. See, what I learned early on in the self-improvement game and it continues today is that many people in the field don't want you to succeed. They talk a big game of abundance mentality, and I have heard them bang on about it at length. But when it comes down to it, they are not interested in whether you are successful spiritually psychologically or whether you are empowered to make a difference or be financially successful.

They just don't care. From what I can tell they have a suite of products, usually information products that they want you to buy. What happens from there is your problem. And one of the biggest concepts, certainly the most popular concept in many ways is self-esteem. If ever you needed evidence that most self-improvement practitioners aren't interested in your success, just listen to what they say about this.

Self Esteem will not save you it is the most damaging concept in self-improvement. And unlike what is somehow magically claimed, it is not innate, and having more is not going to improve your life. It is a sickness, it was touted as a silver bullet and it did not deliver, just ask any educator with an ounce of common sense. There are two main reasons for this, it is conditional and it requires overgeneralisation.

Self-esteem never used to be a thing, ask people who lived through World War two when they first heard of it. It was first mentioned in literature in the late 1800s then started to make its way into the mainstream language in the '60s with the rise of consumerism, and getting more for the self.

Self-esteem by its nature holds that you need to achieve something to feel good about yourself, to accept yourself in reality. Not to feel happier, not to improve your lot in life, but to accept yourself you need to achieve something. If you've ever woken up in the morning and felt like crap for no reason at all, it's likely your self-esteem because you haven't achieved anything yet.

One of the common themes of my system and REBT, in general, is that the three categories of Self, Others, and Circumstance reoccur regularly, such as the case for what is essentially the opposite of self-esteem. No surprise that the opposite of conditional self-acceptance would be Unconditional Self-Acceptance or USA and its follow-on concepts or practices of Unconditional Other Acceptance and Unconditional Life Acceptance.

How does it work? Well, you may already be familiar with the refusal to overgeneralize as one of the assumptions you've got to make. To free yourself from the unhelpful pattern of thinking or cognitive distortion mentioned earlier in the book.

This concept, Unconditional Self-Acceptance in many ways flies directly in the face of the self-improvement movement as most of them think you need more self-esteem. You need to feel good about yourself, it's a global form of rating. As we covered earlier, that involves over-generalising between yourself and your success and thinking that if you just keep pumping yourself up, you'll feel better.

Here's the problem with that, what happens when things don't work out? If you've overgeneralised between yourself and your success, it logically follows that you will overgeneralise between yourself and your setbacks, or failures. You'll engage in many of the cognitive distortions, even if you have high self-esteem, in fact, it's a lot like a see-saw.

Let's consider it like this: you start a new job, and you start getting results early on, for the sake of this analogy you're in sales. I love working with sales teams as this concept can drive them nuts…until they get it. Early on, resistance is high. So, let's say you are a salesperson and you start with a new organisation, great products easy to sell, you get good results early on as I've mentioned, pretty soon your sales manager starts recognising your efforts.

He might say: 'nice one legend' after a while a few more people take notice, they might say 'awesome', then it happens, someone overgeneralises in your favour, your awesome or you're a legend and you're hooked. Sooner or later, you will start to believe the bullshit. Humility goes out the window and you have accepted the overgeneralisation, between yourself and your results as fact. You may now very much believe that you and your results are the same thing, that they are a part of you…somehow.

However, what happens when what you've always done does not achieve the results you've always got. You might not have changed, self esteemers often don't. But the market might've changed, your products or services might've failed to keep up with the market, consumer tastes have changed or the government does something, and changes required of your company make you less competitive.

All of a sudden, your results aren't the same, for whatever reason. You are no longer the legend you once were, now you start to fall behind and God forbid you fail to meet budget one month. Can you see the see-saw starting to shift? All of these things may not even be a result of something you have done. You start to overgeneralise and consider yourself a failure. Beating yourself up when you lose a sale or a valuable client. This in turn makes it harder to get back on the horse each time and just keep trying.

A salesperson in recruiting came to me after a presentation one time and said 'all of this being OK is not going to work for me, I need to be number one!' To which I responded: 'and you can, however not the way you think about it now. If you can separate between your results being the best or number one results in the company or industry and you, being you completely separate you may be on the right path.' Our separation between ourselves and our results comes from refusing to overgeneralise.

You see the problem arises when we overgeneralise and we take that overgeneralisation and affirm it with a global rating. If your self-esteem is high, like the sales example above, and I use sales as an example as I believe we are all salespeople whether we like it or not, you will overgeneralise and globally rate yourself as a legend or something similar. When you have a setback or can't get the same results you label yourself a failure. Both are completely untrue and that's why this concept does not work.

Here's the good news, you are not:
- Your achievements
- Your setbacks
- Your actions
- Your thoughts
- Your emotions
- Your friends or the relationships you have with them
- Your possessions
- Your pets

- Your favourite sporting team
- Or any one of a host of other things that people overgeneralise about.

You are you, a fallible worthwhile human being. Let's not even attempt to define the self, that is a mystical concept that would take years. My father though he has it knocked when I told him the self is too complex to define, he responded 'no it's not I can define it.' When I asked how he said 'me'. Wow, simplified in one fell swoop. So, for the sake of argument if you need to define it, follow my dad's lead and don't read too much into it.

Rating yourself as a fallible worthwhile human being does a couple of useful things, first, it acknowledges that you are capable of making mistakes and second it gets us past the concept of worth. Rating yourself as worthwhile does not work off a sliding scale, it's a constant, you don't stop being worthwhile. This remains a constant and initially, may take some consistency to stick to however over time it can be a comforting reminder, things go bad, don't work out or whatever, I'm still me, a fallible worthwhile human being. Simple.

Instead of being devastated, unbelievable, or whatever refusal to accept reality statement you may have used in the past or routinely hear from others. Compare the two and see how simply being less than preferable and that you are you.

If you want to escape the concept of worth and therefore not allow yourself to take that melodramatic leap. If you consider yourself worthless when something completely external, such as someone's approval of you, which often you cannot influence, and want to change. You can instead, adopt the idea that you have one human's worth and are equal to all others in terms of your humanity.

You're just as human as the next person, that's all we have. It doesn't go up or down. Remember when considering this as a rating scale, I said at the beginning that everything is a choice. You can choose to be this way;

however, it may take some work, some discipline to bring the rest of you around to believing it.

By simplifying and thus removing the rating that we would otherwise do to ourselves, we can focus on the second biggest problem with self-esteem. Overgeneralisation, which is what leads to the rating of ourselves, others, or the circumstance.

It's about refusing to overgeneralize between yourself, your successes, and failures and about finding a space of simply being you. You can stop this over generalisation process by getting yourself to a quiet space away from outside influences; find a quiet room, a place in nature, or outside whilst exercising. Simply say to yourself:

> 'Stop!' (If surrounded by external influences or the noise in your head has not yet caught up with your change in environment… it happens) Say stop in a firm voice, either in your head or out loud.
>
> 'I am not, my successes, not my failures or setbacks.'

You may need to repeat this, I find 3 times seems to do the trick to get you there. Once you address the cause you then need to address the rating. Follow this up with:

> 'I am me, a fallible, worthwhile human being,
> equal to all others in terms of my humanity!'

This might take a few attempts as well but stick with it. What happens with this approach, and it can apply to any type of disciplined thinking that you are attempting to instill, is that your system attempts to reject the new way of thinking. I have to credit Daniel Fryer from the Four Thoughts that F*ck You up with this approach.

Your brain will start to act like a misbehaving child in some instances, this misbehaving child in most instances will start asking why, repeatedly. It's at this stage you have to respond as firmly as possible, feel free to get angry, if necessary, with:

'Because I said so! This is how we are going to think from now on, so get used to it!'

This might also take a few attempts as each person is different, for some of you it might just click and you'll be able to do it. But for those of you for whom it takes some effort and you find yourself drifting back into old habits, this should start to help.

But what's the point of trying to achieve anything? I hear you say, well I'm glad you did. The whole point of trying to achieve anything, and it's a big point, is to simply increase your happiness. We remove the overgeneralisation because it leads to unhappiness and is erroneous, its un true and leads to boosting your ego. Boosting your ego inhibits your awareness of reality by increasing your focus on yourself.

Refusing to do this and instead focusing on feelings of happiness, actually simplifies the situation, increases feelings of gratitude, and promotes humility because you're still the same person. It helps you focus on those who helped you to get there. This is reality-based and helps you to accept life when things do not work out.

It's ok to be upset when things don't work out but it's not ok to beat yourself up. Once again focusing erroneously on yourself and incorrectly labeling yourself as a failure. This is because, going back to challenging how we think, as in this situation when labeling yourself as a failure, you have this as a pretty solid belief. You've most likely bought into this belief very strongly, so we can go back to our three main questions and ask the following.

> **Is it true?** that your entire self is a failure, that every fibre in your being is a worthless desperate human being? Well, no, being a fallible, worthwhile human being who no longer chooses to overgeneralise, this is just a setback. I am understandably unhappy about this but that is where it stops.

> **Does it logically follow?** that because something did not work out, even something that you placed a lot of importance on, make you a failure? It does not follow as it is an extreme exaggeration between what has occurred and who I am. As I have chosen not to respond this way, it will only seek to intentionally make myself more upset to continue with this way of thinking.
>
> **Is it helping?** to rate yourself as a failure? It certainly is not helping and I had better stop using this way of thinking when faced with things that simply don't work out. I can do this by refusing to rate myself as anything other than a fallible worthwhile human being and by rating situations as what they are, unfortunate and nothing more.

The example above is part of a worksheet, with the same questions and answers, and a section with just the questions and blank space below them for you to write your answers to practice and make this easier for you. This is available at www.changeseminars.com/reclaim-handouts.

You may have noticed that the move from Self Esteem to Unconditional Self-Acceptance requires flexibility of thought. Having flexibility in your approach means that you are not a damned worthless human being when things don't work out, but someone who learns by making mistakes. Allowing your acceptance of self to be based on that not only makes the pursuit of whatever you are trying to achieve easier, it is also grounded in reality.

The Good news

Self Esteem, as a global rating system is arbitrary and fairly fixed and requires quite a leap in order to buy into. I'm sure you'd agree when examining overgeneralising and global rating versus unconditional self-acceptance. Flexibly rating and defining your goals by only the basic emotion, happiness for example, when defining our outcome and increasing it as the outcome of the goal. It will require you to stop doing some things but is much less of a leap than claiming failure as your identity when things do not work out or claiming legend status and believing your own BS. Still, after reading this some will hang onto it.

But what about my emotions they say, how can I not feel anything? The reality is that you can actually feel things just the same however, you're doing less damning, less erroneous thinking that doesn't serve you, and experiencing less confusion.

Whilst Self Esteem requires a global rating of the self, this is an arbitrary rating scale. Like blame, it is an end state, one that can lead you to focus on the negative as it requires a view of your entire personhood and belief about everything you are. The good news is, and why I encourage you to adopt a simple easy to demonstrate rating system of yourself, that you are too infinite, too complex and constantly evolving in any way to be accurately defined by a global rating scale.

Acceptance of yourself can be achieved by performing the following experiment. Please hold your hand in front of your face, covering your mouth and your nose. Not touching, about a centimetre in front, and mention the first thing you notice. If that is that you can breathe, you have successfully completed the experiment.

That is all you need to accept yourself. Please indulge me and attempt this experiment first thing in the morning to start your day, you can then relax and remember that achieving things is great and important to increasing your happiness, but that your acceptance of yourself does not need to depend on them.

To help shape your thinking around this approach please observe the following equation:

$$TV + DT = T$$

Equation adapted from Miller (1986).

In Australia, the colloquial term in high school for the simplest mathematics class is 'Maths in the Garden.' To highlight the simplicity of the above equation, it's important to note that the person sharing it with you is a successful graduate of the 1991 Carlingford High School class of Maths in the Garden. Its meaning is as follows:

TV = Tunnel Vision

DT = Dichotomous Thinking, which is all or nothing thinking. Either something is amazing or it sucks, you're driving the Porsche or you're eating out of the dumpster.

T = Trouble

So, your adherence to self-esteem typically follows this equation to illustrate that further allow me to introduce the happy couple:

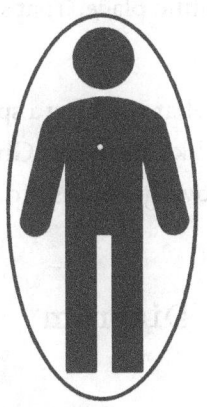 

The dot on the couple is as small as I can make it given the limitations on Microsoft word and is there to represent the size of the problem versus the size of a normal person. If this were accurate it would be so small that you couldn't see it. The reason for this, if someone held a gun to your head and asked you to remember everything that has ever happened to you, what percentage of everything that has happened to you do you think you could recall?

Keep in mind that by the age of 40 you've probably experienced 1 billion things, that is everything you've ever seen, watched, experienced or had done to you. Every word or story you've ever read everything! If you've answered 1%, you're probably starting to get close. I had someone in a webinar recently claim 80% and whilst I'm the last person to tell them they are incorrect giving examples of the sorts of things included in what has occurred in life, he began to see where I was going with this.

The oval shape around the figures is there to represent a global rating that we give ourselves when things do not work out. Given that the extent of something we are overgeneralising about and choosing to beat ourselves about is less than 100th of 1 percent of our entire lives, do you think that is in any way accurate?

You will no doubt be familiar with this couple also, they or a version of them indicate to you there is a toilet in a public place. That's where this concept belongs.

As a way of looking at this is understanding what reaching a space of ok is and how you achieve it, self-esteem is much like a see saw. Given the fact that your Self Esteem is conditional and the overgeneralisation is the part that makes it like this.

Self Esteem See Saw Diagram

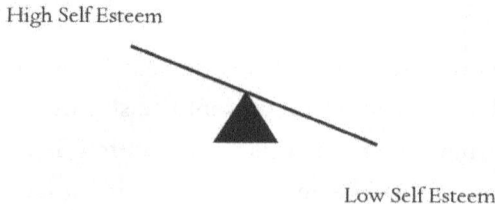

Once you have achieved high self-esteem through say achievements, for example, you complete a task and get a result and you feel good, feel some worth, and generally feel good about yourself. Not happier, although there may be some happiness present, there also might be some relief as well because you can now accept yourself again.

What occurs if that same task the following day doesn't get a positive result? You might have a cold; you might get sinusitis and just not be feeling yourself. If you fail to get the same outcome or if your results start to be less than they were previously and you feel them starting to slip, anxiety can creep in. Then once you finally no longer achieve the same results, as was the case with the example previously about sales, the see-saw swings and you go very quickly from High Self Esteem to Low Self Esteem.

How you get past this and what actually occurs when you refuse to rate yourself unconditionally, you start to get to a space of ok. When you accept yourself because you can breathe, when you rate upsets and setbacks as less than preferable you start to get to what is called a neutral space.

The size of your triangle or base for your see-saw, the fulcrum starts to shrink, and your post indicated by the line starts to level out. Your swings from high self-esteem to low self-esteem aren't as aggressive, you're not beating yourself up as much and when you do, it might be a word, perhaps less intense like 'silly me' as opposed to 'How could I be so stupid? You idiot!'.

To the point where you get your level of unconditional self-acceptance becoming like the solid line below. In the middle of the line is where you sit most of the time and the line above it marks how the line can rise over time leading to a capacity for greater levels of happiness. You can still visit either end of the line temporarily for feeling happier when something works well and unhappy when things don't work out but you are no longer beating yourself up and over generalising.

Unconditional Self-Acceptance Okay Illustration

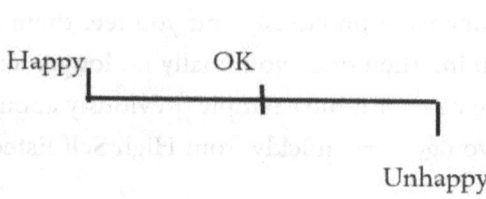

This model is something that I share with participants with audiences, particularly during RUOK day presentations, as it gives them not only a model for understanding where OK sits but also how to go about achieving a state of OK.

CHAPTER 5

UNCONDITIONAL ACCEPTANCE OF OTHERS

'When accepting others as fallible, worthwhile human beings, even if you believe only their mother could form this view is close enough'

So, what about relationships, you probably have noticed that the examples for people and how they achieve self-esteem are based around achievements. Relationships can also be a huge source of self-esteem; we base our acceptance of self around perceived acceptance or lack thereof from societal groups. We try to please others; we mind read by attempting to gauge their thoughts and we place value on this. If a relationship doesn't work out, we grieve.

In order to move beyond this motivator of self-esteem is the same it's just the subject matter that changes. We need to accept that we make mistakes and that we can't please everyone. Or as one of my former bosses in the army once said

'Some people dislike you just because you showed up'

Here is where unconditional acceptance of others or UOA comes into play. Attempting to get self-esteem from relationships is a really good way to drive yourself nuts, given that consistency can be hard to find for people.

Additional things to accept about people and understanding what you can change and what you can't, keeping the model above in mind, this will appear like a series of one liners but it can assist with your self-talk:

- Some people dislike you at first sight, just because you showed up
- Trying to convince someone of your opinion is like trying to teach a pig to sing
- Most people are generally good and don't mean you any harm, in fact, many have enough of their own crap going on.
- Many are not even aware of what you may have done, not done, or think you may have accidentally done to them.
- At the end of the day, you can't please everyone, you've got to please yourself.
- Inferences we make about our personal interactions or how we may appear to others are often never tested against what others recall or reality and should be taken with a grain of salt.

What these phrases pertain to is that beating ourselves up, or considering ourselves as legends because of our positive interactions is often not based in reality and only serves to make life harder if we ignore them.

Studies have also shown that people who are more accepting, I'm not saying that you have to like more things or people than you currently do. But those that accept more, experience lower rates of depression, anxiety and experience higher levels of happiness and well-being. So, there's a lot of supporting evidence for accepting others, yourself, and life unconditionally.

If you remember what you can control from earlier chapters being, what you think, what you feel, what you say, and what you do, and work towards basing your level of concern on those four things you can begin to get to unconditional self-acceptance in your relationships as well as your achievements.

In order to get a baseline of where your current level of acceptance of self, others, or circumstances, there are some handouts on the site **www.changeseminars.com/reclaim-handouts**, to give you a baseline. Look at the unconditional self-acceptance questionnaire and the unconditional acceptance of others scale.

Sensitivities play a very big part. I want to share a situation that I faced a couple of years ago, this highlights the argument for unconditional other acceptance and its importance. We often believe that other people are to blame, we often upset ourselves about other people and their behaviors, and we often have expectations of them or prejudice towards them whether we realize it or not.

I've judiciously applied REBT and the principles of that as long as I've been involved with it. We're talking at least 19 close to 20 years. It's given me a fantastic amount of emotional stability and I've certainly used it on myself. But sometimes I have drawn the line on this is with family and other people close to me. It's often the last place we look to improve. Some of you will work on your relationships with family first, individual situations will differ.

Sometimes the last place you look to improve is your own emotional patch. A couple of years ago my brother and I had an interaction that wasn't positive. Now my brother has made certain lifestyle choices that I don't agree with, but I've done a fair bit of work on myself towards accepting those, or thought I had.

My brother had what felt like an aggressive episode where he decided to have a go at me in a very verbal way with little provocation, in fact, it was completely out of the blue. I was explaining to my father how I had changed real estate management companies for an apartment I own in Melbourne Australia. It's a one-bedroom, in a beautiful art deco building. I am very much an art deco fan and have a soft spot for this property, especially having resided in it when I lived in Melbourne whilst in the army.

The first real estate agent I worked with were very poor communicators and didn't even share with me that they had increased the rent as I'd asked, and also a few other things. I was then berated by my brother who persisted 'If it was me, I'd go in there with my Lawyer blah blah blah!' to which I responded 'For the sake of $20 a week?' This sent him into a rant in front of Harvey, my son. I felt I handled it pretty well in the moment, I had been working on myself and accepting of the fact that without argument or explanation my brother had largely cut us out of his life prior to this. I could feel my anxiety increasing in the days following this incident.

The day after, I remember having a particularly strenuous physical workout pushing myself as hard as I could, almost as though I needed to do it. This, it turned out was my body trying to process what had happened and reduce my defences which led to me becoming quite jittery about what happened. It was an odd experience but so too is the experience of an anxiety disorder, such that I have been diagnosed with.

This sent me back to the psychologist's couch and whilst that was beneficial, and I highly recommend professional help, I can honestly attribute the majority of my being able to reduce that anxiety response to the work that I did next.

One of the things that I kept upsetting myself with was the fact that I had not accepted that he is just a fallible worthwhile human being. That I had to expand my capacity to accept him and the reality that he may never be the brother that I so badly wanted him to be.

Accepting that that's just the way that he is and I'm not going to be able to change him. Despite holding the belief that you can't change people, and they need to want to change themselves, with everyone else in my life it appeared that I hadn't done the work or at least considered that with my brother. As odd as that may sound.

He just kept moving further away, the more that I attempted to include him in my life, and him not accepting that, was providing me with quite a lot of anxiety. By accepting him and understanding that that's just the way that he is. If I actually wanted to hold onto hope that he'd one day come back into my life and he may very well not, I'll have to be patient and accept what comes.

Who in your life have you had difficult relationships with? How could any of those situations be helped by accepting the person in question unconditionally? Where they have strayed from the path you thought they should take, how could you benefit by accepting that circumstances have prevailed either through habits they have had for a long time or behaviours you saw early on that their life might have taken that turn?

You'll remember from the last chapter that the standard that we are choosing to rate ourselves with moving forward, if you accept my challenge and if you are this far in, I expect you're at least prepared to walk into the water with me on my system. The standard that we are now choosing to rate ourselves by is that we are fallible, worthwhile human beings.

That then requires us or at least opens us up to benefit of accepting others the same way. Now I know what you are thinking,

'... but what about that jerk in my office, he's such a you know what!'

Well, if you recall what I mentioned briefly about unconditional self-acceptance in that you don't have to like yourself you only have to accept yourself.

Well at least it's a start you might start to think you are ok, and self-love might grow, but it's not the focus. Accepting yourself is much easier. The same applies to other people, yes including that jerk in the office. By accepting him as a fallible worthwhile human being, even if he is only worthwhile in his mother's eyes. Accepting that someone feels this way is a start.

I used to work with a guy in the military, for the sake of this story we'll call him Steve, who loved doing what we colloquially refer to in Australia as 'taking the piss'. He would bludge, or try to get out of helping others or to get out of doing his bit at every opportunity. He once shared with me that in the 12 months previous to our conversation, in our locker room he had made a bed to sleep on when no one was watching or when he thought he could get away with it. The lockers were very tall which prevented anyone being able to see onto the top of them.

He'd even, intentionally go against the rules that he thought he might only get a slight inconvenience for having committed. I once saw one of the members of his platoon, yell at him for not coming to PT, which we all knew he would take the morning off and go fishing instead. When the team leader yelled at him and it was over, he said, 'well that wasn't as bad as I'd expected.' Indicating he's actually risk assessed what would happen if he took the morning off to go fishing and to him that chewing out was an acceptable risk.

In the military an environment where you need to rely on people potentially as a matter of life and death. Where the hard fought values that are enculturated into you from something as invasive as recruit training, you'd think someone like this would be outed. He'd actually managed to get away with this somehow. But the straw that broke the camel's back for me, was when I felt his lazy attitude was coupled with malice or at least a little jealousy towards others.

In the field outside the wire on my first deployment to Afghanistan, I had in preparation for a mission, looked at everything, or at least thought I had. However, I had forgotten one thing, to double-check and pack a replacement radio handset. The particular item in question, were notoriously unreliable, hence why you always needed a spare one. Anyway, as luck would have it, my handset stopped working in the most annoying of ways, small notches inside the connector that enabled the handset to hold onto the radio had broken off. This meant that I had to stop every time I needed to send or receive communications. Not a good thing on a foot patrol where you are constantly on the move and require regular updates and to be able to get in touch with other support where required in an instant.

As luck would have it our sister platoon, met up with us just as things were going badly and Steve was their radio operator and gladly lent me his spare handset. About 18 months later I was talking to one of the officers from our unit, who was thanking me for a couple of presentations that I did at the school of signals during a demonstration we were holding that week.

Steve, was within ear shot and interjected the conversation by saying 'remember when we were in Afghanistan and you forgot your replacement handset and I had to lend you mine? The timing of this comment could not have been worse and appeared as a deliberate attempt to make me look bad.

Even this despite him being my equivalent of that jerk at the office, on more than one occasion I could accept him as being a fallible person and worthwhile even if it was only in the eyes of his wife.

So as everything assists everything else and the concept of REBT is interoperable with itself, let's consider using our ABCDE model to achieve unconditional acceptance of others. Remembering we can't change them we can only change how we feel about them. Often, we need to appreciate that how they present good, bad, or indifferent is what you're going to get. Asking questions like, is there something about them that you can work with however small? Might be how far you have to search or question in order to be able to do anything productive with them.

ABCDE worksheet for Unconditional Acceptance of Others

(**Example: dealing with people from your past**)

A. Activator: Identify your activator or trigger	B. Belief: (Circle all that apply)	C. Consequence: Identify your feelings and how you behave when triggered by this activator
Thinking about Steve the guy I used to serve with and how he used to put his own comfort above all else	Self **(Others)** Circumstances	**Feelings:** Anger, frustration, annoyed **Behaviour:** Tell him what I think of him, shake my head and speak ill of him

Next ask yourself in a sentence, I get triggered by:

I feel angry when I think of this person and behave in an Angry manner, by telling him what I think of him, shaking my head, and speaking ill of him when in the company of others who feel the same

BECAUSE OF WHAT? Because, in the structured world of the army where integrity is everything to see someone acting so far out of it, is annoying at times and at other times makes me wonder why he is here in the first place

My Belief manifests as: (Circle all that apply):
1. **Demanding** ⟵ circled
2. Catastrophising
3. I can't standititis
4. **Pejorative Putdowns** ⟵ circled

D. Dispute:

1. **Is it true?** Is it true that I need to make myself upset by this person's behaviour? Only when it impacts me and even then, I can minimise this by knowing what to expect and adjusting my expectations of this person accordingly.

2. **Does it logically follow?** Does it logically follow that I need to choose to get upset by this person's behaviour? Obviously not and I'd be better served by accepting that people like this person exist and that this guy just happens to be our jack/lazy individual.

3. **Is it helping?** Is it helping that I upset myself about this person? Obviously not and I'd better do what I can to find the good that this person brings and do my best to focus on that instead.

E. Enforce your preferences.

Of course, I'd prefer that this guy didn't behave this way, I wish that he didn't try to pull me down when I was getting a compliment and I'd very much like it if he worked to the same set of values that we all did. But he doesn't and probably never will and that's ok. He does have some good qualities; he obviously cares about his country the same as I do or he wouldn't be there. And it takes different strokes to move the world as they say.

Believe it or not, I hadn't actually gone into that level of detail over this person, prior to completing the above table and that felt great to do. In fact, recalling that memory and working through the ABCs removed some of the stress that I was feeling, which recalling that guy brought back up. I know it will work for you, remember if you want your own copy of the worksheet to scan the QR code on the copyright page at the start of this book. Or visit the site: **www.changeseminars.com/reclaim-handouts**

Unconditional Acceptance of Life or ULA

The third part of the Unconditional Acceptance triangle is unconditional acceptance of life, or unconditional life acceptance ULA. Much of this comes from inserting life and the circumstances into what we have already discussed. Accepting that circumstances transpire and the outcome is a circumstance that for whatever reason either provides you with some adversity or a situation that is not conducive to you is a big step.

If you recall how beliefs manifest that we discussed previously: demandingness, catastrophisation, awfulising and pejorative putdowns. There is an amount of lack refusal to accept what is occurring and how life is playing out in all demands that things are not as they are. Whether it's demanding that you not be asked to present in public, demand that others not disrespect you, or cut you off in traffic or any one of a number of things (insert your most recent upset here).

Learning to accept life unconditionally can go a long way to reducing our demandingness and our overall upset. Just like USA and UOA, we need to remember that accepting circumstances does not mean you have to be resigned to them. In fact, quite the opposite. But what it will do is allow you to make plans and change your circumstances in an emotionally lighter, more neutral space and make more intelligent choices for yourself as well. Remember, as the saying goes, 'High emotion equals low intelligence'.

Not that REBT with its origins in Stoic Philosophy is anti-emotions, far from it. It's unfortunate that being considered 'Stoic' in today's world is characterized by showing little emotion. The stoics actually thought very differently about emotions and just like with REBT, sought to get your emotions to work for you and not against you, as can certainly feel like what happens when emotions are high Robertson (2020).

Unconditional Life Acceptance and its requirement to accept reality is an opportunity for you to check-in with yourself and see how optimistic you actually are. Not blindly optimistic as that in my opinion is not optimism at all but rather being delusional and using optimism as the thing to be delusional about. As we know from the research that optimists cope better with setbacks and difficulties, deal better with grief, and score better across the board on all indicators of psychological stress.

If you haven't already, do a YouTube search for Jocko Willink's 'Good' you'll be glad you did. This video goes a long way towards doing something the military has been advising us for years about unconditional life acceptance and dealing with difficult or adverse circumstances. Embracing the suck.

CHAPTER 6

AFFECTING YOUR LANGUAGE TO FACILITATE LESS EXTREMES

'Our Words Create Our Reality'

As you may have noticed there are certain language patterns and terms of phrase or simply words that are used when overgeneralising versus, speaking and acting rationally.

This is where we learn further ways to reduce our levels of concern down to what we can actually control. You may remember the diagram below, from the considerations section of the book. It represents where these circles sit for most people. Reducing the emotional weight of the words we use, helps us to focus on what we can control. One of the four things that you can control is what you say. If you reduce the words you use to reflect a less emotive and melodramatic view of the world with this one discipline, you are reducing your circle of concern and bringing it ever closer to your circle of control.

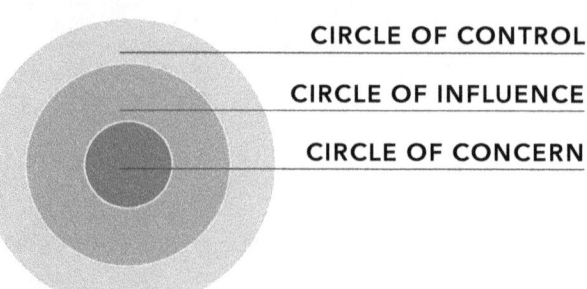

For someone prone to irrational thinking and extreme overgeneralisation, words like devastating when something goes wrong are common and life-changing when things go well. The reality is that these people can become a bit like either the boy who cried wolf or just a pain in the ass. I've had people tell me that they can't live without their emotions. They are often referring to extremes of emotion, they claim 'without emotion life isn't worth living!' however what they are doing is incorrectly judging, attempting to get back some sort of control over your emotions so that they serve you, this is instead of letting them run your life in a completely self-indulgent way. But there may be no helping some people.

Keeping in line with the quote at the start of this chapter, our words to some extent really do create our reality. It relates in many ways to how to help you to achieve a more rational and therefore happier existence. This can be achieved by practicing some simple language disciplines. Now I know what most people might be thinking, 'oh no not discipline!' Well as I explained earlier, Jocko Willink was right 'Discipline Equals Freedom.'

I must follow that by mentioning this he also claims it's a balance to much discipline equals no freedom and not enough discipline equals very little freedom also Willink & Babin (2018). Right now, if you're reading this you can rest assured that I was often credited as being the least army person when I served. Meaning I didn't have any of the standard military-type attitudes prevalent at least in the Australian army. However, despite my relaxed approach to life and the flexibility that achieving anything requires, an appreciation of small disciplines is extremely useful in order to help you stick to your desired outcomes.

If you want financial freedom, you need to adhere to financial disciplines, if you want to be able to perform great physical feats of acrobatics, yoga, or fitness you need physical discipline. The same holds if you want your language to assist you in becoming more rational, and experience greater levels of happiness, some level of discipline around this is also a massive help. In fact, having a disciplined approach to your language is one of the biggest ways to help ensure you get the most out of this system.

What does that look like? Below is a diagram that I drew for a client recently, faithfully reproduced within the limitations of Microsoft word. Usually when drawing this on a flip chart it will have red in the 100% category, green for 50%, and blue or black for the 75% to indicate a transition from the extreme zone of 100% bad.

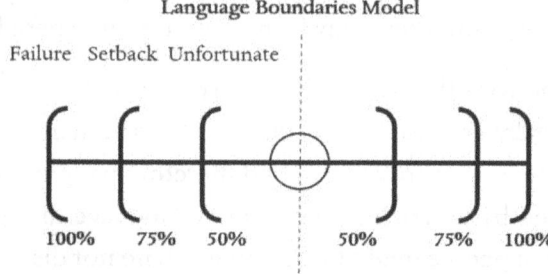

What you'll typically find by reducing your language to less extreme terms is that it enables your capacity to not over generalise between yourself and your successes and your failures, making life a lot easier. An example of this; with my client Mike, who I recently used this diagram with to explain how I wanted him to start reducing the extremities of his language.

For almost 12 years he claimed to have considered his not speaking up to question a decision, that in hindsight would've prevented a tragic failure and loss of life in a training accident, a devastating failure. To paint the picture and give you more context, Mike had an irrational belief about himself, and whilst he had moved past demandingness about the event, he was still catastrophising that it was 100% bad. This made him difficult to be around when he started talking about it with friends as Mike had never come to terms with the situation.

He also had a secondary belief about others, blaming the team leader who made the decision, for changing the plans last minute. The belief about himself was strongest but not by much, the belief Mike had about himself being a failure or having failed was 10 out of 10 in terms of how bad he viewed what had happened. The negative belief about the team leader having failed was 9 out of 10.

As these beliefs take time to work through, I made a point of not rushing through the process of giving up his stinking thinking too soon. This is evident in the graded reduction of intensity from 100% to 75% to 50%. In the first session, I drew the diagram and asked Mike to go from failure in terms of his descriptive language to setback. I did this by the use of a concept called REI, or Rational Emotive Imagery.

I asked Mike to close his eyes and imagine they are at the location where the accident took place, and consider how he feels when things are 100% bad, a failure or worse, in fact, I asked him to make it worse in his mind, to move it to 11 or 12 out of 10 in terms of how bad it is. This was useful as it helped him to see that it could indeed be worse and that he is capable of moving the scale.

Next, I asked Mike to imagine himself, still with his eyes closed using REI, reducing the severity of the situation and instead of viewing it as a setback, significant as it may be but still viewing it as a setback. I asked him to share what he was saying to himself whilst he was doing this. Phrases such as 'I can do this' and 'I am doing this' are common.

From there with the 50% indication of labeling the situation that occurred all that time ago as being less than preferred, unfortunate or regrettable as depicted on the diagram. I explained to Mike that we wouldn't go there in that session but that we would cover that in our next session. This was important as it gave him a goal to shoot for and that he could consolidate what we had just done by completing the REI activity 3 times a day until we next met.

Given that this activity takes less than a minute to complete, it's achievable and helped him to make the leap of faith required for the approach to take hold and become part of his everyday thinking. You can use this to reduce your descriptive language and reduce the intensity of a particularly stressful or upsetting event.

Simply start with the event in mind, and be clear from your ABC model where you are up to with it. Do you consider it 10 out of 10 or 100% bad, awful or terrible, or something lighter? Remember it needs to be 7 out of 10 or worse. Next, determine where you want to take the intensity level of how you are feeling about the scenario and the descriptive language you wish to use. For most people starting out, I encourage you not to attempt to take it from 10 to 5, you can attempt this of course if you wish, but getting it to move to a more manageable level of intensity is the first goal. If you have held on to negative feelings around this upset, for months or even years it may be easier to reduce it by smaller intervals.

Next, close your eyes and imagine yourself reducing the intensity, try attempting to change the colour you see, the emotions, the pictures you see, or something that naturally occurs in your mind's eye. It may be something unrelated that you see like a scale with a red level that goes down, steam might come off as it cools or whatever you come up with. Then ask yourself to put the feeling of achieving this into words or simply tune in to your internal dialogue as you do it. Finally re-lable how you feel about the situation with your reduced, less intense, or less dramatic term.

You may wish to use the term that you will now describe how you intend to feel about the situation as part of your visualization. Next, practice it no less than 3 times a day for the next few days before attempting to reduce it further. Once you are well-practiced in this, reducing it all the way from 10 to 5 or 6 can be done in one go and may occur quickly and easily.

I took Mike from 7.5 out of 10 in terms of negative intensity using a different type of approach but still within the realms of REI. Where in the first session I asked him to imagine himself seeing the intensity reduce and leaving it largely up to him to determine the imagery that he used. For the next session, I directed Mike by the use of very specific imagery. Where I attempted above to give you examples to get you started, I gave him one example.

In the session, once Mike had closed his eyes, I asked him to return to the scenario, that he had been ruminating over all of this time. When the particular incident occurred, I asked him to see himself falling from the sky, imagining briefly at the start of the imagery when the incident occurred to feel the intensity of the negative emotion of the situation. As he fell from the sky, Mike was to imagine that he was about to land on an iceberg, whilst he was falling almost like skydiving but with no parachute so to imagine falling quite quickly to pass through the new description of the situation and the unfortunate result as a setback and to feel that totally.

Once he landed on the iceberg, to feel any remaining intensity to come off him as steam and to accept the new definition. As the iceberg is quite comfortable, in the imagery process at least, and to feel that intensity calming right down to 5 out of 10, Seeing his part in the situation as unfortunate and at worst regrettable becomes more achievable.

Use of Imagery and explaining how to do it yourself combines both the language change and the introduction of the discipline to help with a negative situation from your past. Changing up many of your commonly used phrases or terms does not have to be that involved and can in fact be done with a few choices and committing to saying them, with a bit of practice in your everyday language.

This can be done with a simple word exercise of looking at a list of emotive terms and choosing to use less intense synonyms instead. It's important that you chose synonyms that you believe you are likely to use or that you like the sound of, to increase your chances of success. If you fall off and go back to old language patterns, that's fine we learn by making mistakes so just have another go.

If you are sitting on the fence or are skeptical of this approach, walk into the water with me on this. Let's assume you were asked to do one of the most frightening things that most people can think, that's right I am about to use public speaking again. Just imagine you've been asked to present somewhere at short notice in front of people you hardly know, a group of total strangers and you are freaking out. Close your eyes and imagine the situation, the location, and any other visual things about the situation that you can. If you are not a visual person, engage your other senses and imagine from that point of view. Also, think about how you are responding physiologically, are you shaking, do you have a dry mouth or sweaty palms?

Next think of all the words you would use to describe the situation and let them flood into your mind, words like frightening, scary, upsetting may all come up for you. Next imagine you can actually do it, let's imagine for the sake of this visualization you have been presenting on this topic for years and are considered an expert in the field, how does it feel now? How are you describing it to yourself? What are the words you are using? If they are different from the first part of the visualization, how did the change in descriptive words help?

Reigning your language in tighter boundaries works with that approach, however over time and once you commit to the new language and successfully use them, you don't go through the negative part like you may have experienced at the beginning of the visualization. I have used this technique with public speaking students when I used to teach public speaking and found that using the less emotive language helped to motivate reducing the intensity of the emotions felt when people were extremely nervous, or even just a little bit nervous.

In my military career, a time when Australia and in fact the coalition partners of the United States, the United Kingdom, Canada, and many others were at war in Afghanistan it was not uncommon to attend funerals. Despite Australia's comparatively small loss of troops on the battlefield 41 to be exact, at the time I was a member of the Army unit that shouldered the majority of these deaths.

It was not uncommon to have known or been on course at some stage with one of these brave warriors and in my case, I knew four of them very well having been part of the same company. How I was able to reconcile psychologically and thus come out of the period of grief using the techniques affecting my language outlined in this chapter is worth noting. The same technique I was also able to use to great effect in dealing with the suicides of mates since retiring as well.

Instead of labeling and thus interpreting these deaths as devastating, which it would be fair to claim for the families or battle buddies of these individuals it was. I simply labeled them by the core emotion of being sad, extremely sad in most cases mind you but sad nonetheless. Why only sad and not devastating? Well because sadness passes, devastation requires significant rebuilding and may even be something you can never fully recover from.

Below is a list of common negative emotive terms and their synonyms, please go through and circle the ones that you use regularly and underline the replacement ones that you will commit to changing. You can do it with any negative or overly emotive terms to bring your words into less emotive bounds, here is a good place to start. As you'll see some of them are more intense than the ones that have been highlighted so choose wisely.

Synonyms For Negative Emotive Terms

afraid	anxious	apprehensive	ashamed
cowardly	frightened	guilty	horrified
paralyzed	petrified	scared	shocked
shy	skittish	startled	terrified
terrorized	timid	troubled	worried
aggressive	bellicose	belligerent	combative
hawkish	merciless	presumptuous	pugnacious
ruthless	self-assertive	angry	enraged
exasperated	furious	incensed	indignant
livid	mad	outraged	wrathful
annoyed	asinine	bored	disgusted
dullish/dull	obtuse	peeved	riled
vexed			
evil	abusive	baneful	contaminated
contemptible	corrupt	cruel	demonic
depraved	despicable	devilish	diabolic
ferocious	fiendish	fierce	heartless
hellish	infernal	inimical	malicious
nasty	nefarious	nether	perfidious
putrefied	savage	scrupulous	sinister
sneaky	spiteful	spoiled	tainted
treacherous	venal	vile	villainous
wicked			
frustrated	balked	disappointed	discontented

AFFECTING YOUR LANGUAGE TO FACILITATE LESS EXTREMES

foiled	thwarted	nervous	alarmed
anxious	apprehensive	cautious	concerned
confused	conspicuous	disturbed	doubtful
insecure	irritable	panicked	perturbed
suspicious			
pathetic	affecting	agitating	lamentable
piteous	pitiful	poignant	stirring
touching	quarrelsome	blatant	boisterous
cantankerous	clamorous	conspicuously	contentious
cross	deafening	disagreeable	fretful
hysterical	jealous	litigious	mean
mean-spirited	militant	nasty	noisy
offensively	ornery	peevish	pugnacious
rambunctious	recalcitrant	renitent	roisterous
strident	testy	touchy	truculent
unpleasant	vociferous		
sad	bleak	dejected	depressed
desolate	dingy	discouraged	dismal
doleful	dreary	forlornly	gloomy
glum	grievous	grim	heartbroken
lonely	lugubrious	melancholic	miserable
mopish	morose	mournful	Poor
seamy	somber	sordid	sorrowful
sulky	sullen	temperamental	unfortunate
unhappy	wistful	wretched	

stubborn	adamant	hardheaded	inflexible
obdurate	obstinate	relentless	unyielding
terrible	abhorrent	abominable	appalling
awful	bizarre	calamitous	dire
disastrous	dreadful	fearful	formidable
freakish	frightful	ghastly	grotesque
gruesome	heinous	horrible	horrid
lurid	odious	painful	terrifying
tragic			

The above list of words was put together by **www.smart-words.org**, there is a copy of the list available by clicking on the QR code or by going to **www.changeseminars.com/reclaim-handouts**.

What the above list illustrates is that in the process of shaping some of the language you use it's not a process of dumbing down your language. Quite the contrary, it involves expanding your vocabulary and, in many cases, it involves using more complex and therefore more intelligent choices.

You might notice public figures and politicians tend to use terms that would fit into what we have discussed in this chapter. Speechwriters are well aware of the power of language and how keeping language from being too extreme can impact how people respond to their words.

The biggest benefit to shaping the language we use to facilitate less extreme responses is that it aids in creating and maintaining a space of okay. For many being in a space of okay, is short-lived before the next catastrophe hits. Using techniques like those outlined in this chapter can help you to stay there for longer and to right the ship as it were, faster when navigating an emotional storm.

CHAPTER 7

FRUSTRATION

'The biggest issue for many of us, concerning frustration, involves a refusal to deal with it, resulting in low frustration tolerance.'

Frustration can be defined as 'a feeling of being upset or annoyed as a result of being unable to change or to achieve something.'

Frustrations can come in many forms you can be frustrated with your career or your relationships if the future looks uneventful or uninteresting. Have you had a special occasion or a holiday rained out? Have you had trouble losing weight only to put it back on? Have you had difficulty breaking bad habits, such as smoking or drinking too much? Do you compare yourself to others and get frustrated when they get all of the breaks and you don't seem to? Have you ever found putting together a simple child's toy or flat pack furniture confusing? Have you had someone cut you off in traffic? Do you have more household chores or unpleasant routines than you would prefer? Are you dissatisfied with your financial status?

Some of these things that frustrate us seem like they are out of our control, usually it's because the answer is more complex than we at first thought, or we just haven't come across the right advice. Whatever the reason, it brings us back to our circles of control, but many of these frustrations can be attributed to the fact that they feel out of our control and we'd like for them to be within our control.

Let's briefly revisit what we can control and how that might pertain to dealing without frustrations. Below are the four things we can control and an example of how we can take action in the case of each of them to bring about some outcome

What we say – changing the language we use, bringing it into more rational boundaries as outlined in the previous chapter.

What we feel – using the ABC model can help us to feel more rational more of the time and hence work through our frustrations easier.

What we think – the above point also pertains to our thoughts; however, we can also adopt more supportive processes to assist our thinking, developing standards for ourselves, and adhering to values.

What we do – this can be specific to the particular frustration that appears out of our control. Not happy with your financial situation? Start educating yourself on financial matters, read everything you can. Not happy with your relationships? Start learning how to relate better with others and so on.

The outcomes of these things might not happen quickly, but they will start to make a difference over time.

The above examples whilst all common are just a snapshot of what can frustrate us. Whilst it's impossible to get rid of frustration entirely and really why would you want to as frustration, believe it or not, does have some upsides.

When you make the call to initiate some real change in your life because you have decided enough is enough, that can be motivated by frustration. As a parent, if you're getting frustrated with a daycare provider for your kids and decided there has to be a better way.

I can recall when in my early 30's not satisfied with some of my life choices up to that stage. Frustration was an everyday occurrence, I had a job I hated, couldn't get my career back on track. I was working as a security guard trying to grow my speaking business, I fit into a few of the sources of frustration listed above. I was dissatisfied with my financial status; I was starting to develop some bad habits as a result and the future wasn't looking good if I attempted to continue the way that I was.

My work was becoming more frustrating, dealing with drunks and people on lifestyle substances. The days off that I originally had free to work on my business, were more and more being taken up with attempting to deal with the stress and frustration of my situation and not trying to pull myself out of it. Or knowing how. Time for working on what I hoped would take me out of my situation seemed to be growing less and less, I felt trapped and helpless an increasing amount of the time.

For me, the solution was not obvious despite it staring me in the face. It wasn't until a mate came to visit on his way to his next posting with the army that the penny finally dropped. He suggested just doing a 4-year contract with the army, to that point I hadn't considered serving in the regular army despite, somehow hoping to return as a reservist. Feeling as if I made a mistake by not going on deployment overseas when offered a few years earlier and was constantly noticing similarities between my security job and skills I had developed in my previous army career.

One of the big mistakes I thought that I had made was thinking that I knew better when offered to deploy. Now I realised I didn't, that's why my mate's suggestion had such relevance. Not only did it come from a place of genuine concern, but I realised it was time I stopped taking my advice.

In the end, I started to realise before my mate's timely suggestion that to get where I needed to be that I needed more life experience. Joining the army then became the way to achieve this. Whilst it's not for everyone, it was the best move for me.

That's not to say resuming my military career was the antidote to frustration, often instead it created a whole new set of frustrations.

However, it helped give me something to sink my teeth into, something to test my theory and system and put myself to the test on the world stage and escape feeling trapped and directionless.

What we are therefore seeking to do in this section is to learn to bring frustration into more manageable bounds. With our already well-practiced ABC model that is possible, although frustration does have some unique qualities over other, negative emotions.

By improving your ability to deal with frustrations, you're going to free up yourself to have more time and energy to do the things that you'd rather be doing, which in turn helps to develop a relaxed sense of confidence and control over your life's stressors.

But let's start with acknowledging where you are, which is the first step of our approach to frustration.

The following frustration awareness inventory is adapted from William J Knaus' book 'How to Conquer Your Frustrations' whilst only scratching the surface is a good place to start to identify sources of your frustration. There is also a downloadable version at www.changeseminars.com/reclaim-handouts or by scanning the QR code at the front of the book. Answer the questions below as either true or false to the best of your ability.

Frustration Awareness Inventory

1. I feel satisfied with my career.   T   F
2. I have at least one poor habit.   T   F
3. I get to meetings on time.   T   F
4. I keep my life so well-organized that I have very little stress.   T   F
5. I don't manage my finances well.   T   F
6. I often want to get away from it all.   T   F
7. I feel frustrated when I can't find something.   T   F

8. I remain calm if I can't find a parking place. T F
9. I feel frustrated when I can't find something interesting to do. T F
10. Lateness doesn't bother me. T F
11. I rarely get into conflict with my neighbors. T F
12. When I'm stuck in traffic, I make constructive use of my time. T F
13. I usually get my work completed on schedule. T F
14. I get bugged by delayed deliveries, confusing instructions, and other matters that slow me down. T F
15. I get frustrated when I have to wait in line. T F
16. I feel tolerant of people who borrow items and don't return them. T F
17. I feel frustrated if I don't know the answer to a question. T F
18. I feel unhappy with my usual daily routine. T F
19. I have a quick temper. T F
20. I don't get bogged down by detail. T F

If you circled T for numbers 1, 3, 4, 8, 11, 12, 13, 16, and 20, and F for numbers 2,5, 6,7,9,10,14,15,17,18, and 19, you have few, if any, frustrations.

The inventory results may provide some clues as to whether you experience ongoing frustrations in important sectors of your life. If you answered true to any of situations 2, 5, 6, 10, 18, or 19, and false to any of situations 1, 3, 4, 11, 13, or 20, you may have identified an ongoing frustration problem worth exploring.

The remaining items reflect your tolerance for normally frustrating circumstances. If you answered true to items 7, 9, 14, and 17, and false to items 8, 12, and 16, you feel frustrated by events that most people find frustrating.

Frustration is one we all struggle with from time to time, once you have mastered or at least have begun to practice what has been covered so far, the approach to frustration outlined in this chapter makes more sense. If you have skipped over any section of this book, I encourage you to go back and finish it before reading this chapter. The approach we are about to take to deal with frustration will make more sense.

If we go back to our circles of control diagram you may remember previously, it's very easy to feel your loss of control when in a frustrated state of mind and often we can feel frustrated by what other people do or don't do. That's because we are choosing to be concerned about these things. But we are stubborn individuals at times and it might not feel like a choice, let this idea sit with you for a while first if need be.

There are three major ways to eliminate frustration.

1. Physical Exercise
2. Changing your way of thinking
3. Changing your habits

Physical exercise is important as it helps to get rid of the negative energy that can be stored in the body. Although regular exercise is highly recommended, I believe it needs to be combined with changing your habits and way of thinking as a coping mechanism for frustration. Despite doing my best to exercise 5 to 6 times per week and encouraging members of my Facebook group and Meetups to join me on my obstacle race adventures. As I am not an exercise physiologist or personal trainer, I do not recommend any specific exercise program. Happy to share what I do for exercise, if interested, via any of my contact channels.

Changing your way of thinking and your habits is the main advice offered with this book and my program. With the above points in mind and REBT more specifically, I have developed a 5 point system, for working through your frustrations.

The 5 parts are:
1. Acknowledge your frustration
2. Analyse it through the ABC model
3. Immerse yourself in it
4. Use your disputing skills to address it
5. Make it a habit

The first step is to acknowledge your frustration. This might sound obvious, but if you've read the section on the power of accepting reality, you'll be aware of how important this is. Not forcing yourself to be happy about the fact that you are feeling frustrated but, accepting that circumstances have transpired, people have acted or you have made a mistake that triggers you, and you have responded in this way.

The next step is to analyse what is occurring through an ABC framework. This is simply what you should be doing by now almost automatically if you have been practicing what we have covered so far. Below is a table and example to prompt you, if you have not yet completed one of these or would rather not have to draw your own check out **www.changeseminars.com/reclaim-handouts** or scan the QR code at the front of the book for your free copy.

A. Activator:	B. Belief:	C. Consequence:
Identify your activator or trigger	(Circle all that apply)	Identify your feelings and behaviours when triggered by this activator
Getting stuck in a traffic jam	⊙Self⊙ Others ⊙Circumstances⊙	**Feelings:** Frustration **Behaviour:** Hit the steering wheel, stop others from getting into the lane in front of me

> **When I get stuck in a** traffic jam, I feel frustrated and behave in a selfish and aggressive manner towards other drivers
>
> **BECAUSE OF WHAT?**
>
> Because I need to get where I am going and I bet it was some idiot just like them whose selfish decision led us all to this traffic jam. I bet they'll be like every other loser on this road if it is a breakdown and take extra time to stop traffic and just stare at whoever is parked on the side of the road. This situation is totally unfair if only the government would make these roads four lanes instead of two. Why don't they have any foresight? I bet they made this tunnel 2 lanes on purpose.

For the sake of this example, I merged the cell for the because of what question, partly to include as many frustration statements about driving as I could think of and also because this section is not including a disputation or further analysis of how beliefs manifest.

The next step is immersion and here is where we start to deviate from what we have covered previously. In other forms of upset, we do not always have the opportunity, due to the nature of the emotion, to immerse ourselves in it. Not so with frustration, just about any time is a good or at least available time to go and frustrate yourself in order to practice this approach.

What I am encouraging you to do is to complete a low frustration tolerance task. The rules for this task are simple, choose something that frustrates you and do it. Set yourself a goal for its completion, how long will you take?

Some examples include going driving in peak hour when you don't have to go anywhere, driving behind a bus, going to a supermarket selecting one item to purchase, finding the longest line you can, and waiting at the end. If anyone offers to let you in, politely refuse, in fact, you could let others in front of you. Try this for 20 minutes.

One of my clients sits on a particular side of politics, he chose to watch a television program with two people from the side of politics he doesn't follow and tried to see their side of things. If you have a particular pet frustration, one that may have come up in the frustration inventory above, find a way to expose yourself to that.

I personally dislike driving around a suburb near my house with winding roads and continuous corners, so bad is this area that someone who lives there can wear out their car tyres in less than half the recommended time. To give you an idea of how bad, I used to have a client who lived in this suburb and we would routinely complain about the place. I have chosen to frustrate myself so much with this location that when looking for a house to buy, my wife and I always scroll straight past any of the houses there. For my online mentoring program, I did a 5 minute instructional on driving through that same area as a low frustration tolerance task.

This should get you well in the zone of what frustrates you, now that you have already documented what the activator is, how you typically feel and behave, it's now time to start disputing. We'll now return to our form and continue with the process. Remember if you haven't attempted to determine how your beliefs manifest in the situation before disputing, that will then make it more effective as you know which habits you are working through, as well as which unhelpful thought patterns you are helping to eliminate.

Getting to that level of detail whilst it might seem complex can actually be incredibly rewarding and help you to work your way through what is upsetting you at a deeper level. Once you practice this more, it will allow you to get completely clear and learn to accept life's inevitabilities if that is something you get frustrated about.

A. Activator: Identify your activator or trigger Getting stuck in a traffic jam	B. Belief: (Circle all that apply) (Self) Others (Circumstances)	C. Consequence: Identify your feelings and Behaviour when triggered by this activator **Feelings:** Frustration **Behaviour:** Hit the steering wheel, stop others from getting into the lane in front of me

When I get stuck in a traffic jam, I feel frustrated and behave in a selfish and aggressive manner towards other drivers

BECAUSE OF WHAT?

Because I need to get where I am going and I bet it was some idiot just like them whose selfish decision led us all to this traffic jam. I bet they'll be like every other loser on this road if it is a breakdown and take extra time to stop traffic and just stare at whoever is parked on the side of the road. This situation is totally unfair if only the government would make these roads four lanes instead of two. Why don't they have any foresight? I bet they made this tunnel 2 lanes on purpose.

My Belief, therefore, manifests as (Circle all that apply):
1. (Demanding)
2. (Catastrophising)
3. (I can't standititis)
4. Pejorative putdowns

D. Dispute:

1. **Is it true?** Is it true that these people are losers? Most likely not, they are just trying to get through their day like I am. Is it true that whatever has caused the traffic jam and whoever is involved is an idiot? No, it's not, we all make mistakes and if someone is at fault, I would expect that they did not intend for this to occur.

2. **Does it logically follow?** Does it logically follow that I should behave in a selfish and aggressive manner toward other drivers when stuck in a traffic jam? No, it does not we are all just trying to get somewhere.

3. **Is it helping?** Is it helping to carry on like this and blame the government for the inadequate roads? No, as that's akin to blaming an inanimate object or the weather. There is very little that can be done or achieved by carrying on in this way. I'd be much better served listening to an audiobook or podcast.

E. Enforce your preferences:

Of course, I'd prefer that traffic jams didn't happen, that people drove responsibly, didn't rubberneck at the side of breakdowns and the roads were 10 lanes across. But the reality is something different and I'd better accept it if I am to be less disturbed and enjoy my driving into the future.

The final point to our 5 part approach to dealing with our frustrations, and I say 'ours' as I am prone to them as well, is to make it a habit. Hence the point of the worksheet. A version of the worksheet is also available on the site. **www.changeseminars.com/reclaim-handouts** or by scanning the QR code at the front of the book.

A note about joining the military

As my experience and time in the military is mentioned throughout this book, I figure it's worth sharing some thoughts about whether or not you should join. I get a lot of guys approach me when they learn about my service and explain how they nearly joined or almost did then something happened, they got injured, got accepted to university or something else took off. If that's you, obviously life had other plans, and it's ok. You may be better off for having not joined.

That might sound odd coming from someone who got as much out of the military as I did personally. But I've seen it many times, it's not for everyone. So don't think that joining the military will solve all of your problems, they're still going to be there. But for some of you reading this it might. My only advice if you are going to make a career out of the military is to decide what you want to get out of it, set an exit date, and develop a strategy for getting out as soon as you can. If on the other hand, you choose to make a long-term career out of it that's ok also, just make sure it's what you really want.

CHAPTER 8

HEALTHY NEGATIVE VS UNHEALTHY NEGATIVE EMOTIONS

> 'High Emotion, Equals Low Intelligence'
> —BLAIR SINGER

In this chapter, we are going to be looking at emotions, no surprises there. However, what may have appeared as a typo, when reading the name of the chapter is actually true. One of the ways REBT differs from other forms of CBT is that it acknowledges the difference between healthy and unhealthy negative emotions. Part of what will be covered is how simply attempting to be positive in the face of unhealthy negative emotions may not only not work, but it may represent denial or a distraction from what is occurring. We will also look at and discuss the rational alternatives of healthy negative emotions.

By holding a healthy negative belief, we are less disturbed and able to think in more constructive ways. Our perception is more realistic, which enables us to deal with a complex situation, which may trigger the negative situation, and hence our belief in a problem-solving approach.

This approach to emotions is consistent with reducing extreme language mentioned earlier and the names of healthy negative emotions reflect this. You may recall, that I discussed an example of what we are about to learn in more detail, the approach to describing emotions that I used when dealing with the grief of losing mates on the battlefield. That it was just sad, very sad perhaps, but sad nonetheless and sadness passes over time.

Unhelpful patterns of thinking also known as cognitive distortions mentioned throughout this book are also at play, with unhealthy negative emotions. Three that come to mind are: jumping to conclusions, mind reading, and overgeneralisation. These, as we know are most likely to occur when holding rigid or extreme negative beliefs about something that has occurred and are important to be aware of if you are experiencing an unhealthy negative emotion and would like to work towards replacing it with its healthy alternative. You may notice other unhelpful patterns of thinking as their influence is pervasive across many different types of emotional upset.

Let's now look at all of the unhealthy negative emotions and their healthy counterparts. In this section adopted from Dryden (1999), we are going to discuss not only each emotion and its alternative but also the inferences for those emotions both negative and positive, the thinking patterns that result from those emotions, and how we tend to behave. This follows how we respond when we have those emotions, we think a certain way and we respond physically. Including the inference that we make in relation to ourselves, will make sense as we work with replacing an unhealthy negative emotion with a healthy one as you can see with greater clarity where the emotion is coming from.

Healthy Negative Vs Unhealthy Negative Emotions Table
Adapted from Dryden(1999).

Unhealthy	Healthy
Anxiety	Concern
Inference: Threat or danger	
Thoughts: Overestimates negative features of the threat Underestimates ability to cope with the threat Creates an even more negative threat in one's mind Has more task-irrelevant thoughts than in concern	**Thoughts** Views the threat realistically A realistic appraisal of ability to cope with the threat Does not create an even more negative threat in one's mind Has more task-relevant thoughts than in anxiety
Behaviours To withdraw physically from the threat To withdraw mentally from the threat To ward off the threat (through superstitious behaviour) To tranquilize feelings To seek reassurance	**Behaviours** To face up to the threat To deal with the threat realistically

Unhealthy	Healthy
Depression	Sadness
Inference: Loss or failure	
Thoughts: Only sees negative aspects of the loss or failure Thinks of other losses and failures that one has experienced Thinks one is unable to help self (helplessness) Only sees pain and blackness in the future (Hopelessness)	**Thoughts:** Able to see both negative and positive aspects of the loss or failure Less likely to think of other losses and failures than when depressed Able to self-help Able to look towards the future with hope
Behaviours To withdraw from reinforcements To withdraw from oneself To create an environment consistent with feelings To attempt to terminate feelings of depression in self-destructive ways	**Behaviours:** To express feelings about the loss or failure and talk about these to significant others To seek out reinforcements after a period of mourning

Unhealthy	Healthy
Anger	Anger
Inference: Frustration, self, or others breaks a personal rule, threat to self-esteem.	
Thoughts: Overestimates the extent to which the other person acted deliberately Sees malicious intent in the motives of others Self seen as definitely right; other(s) seen as definitely wrong Unable to see other person's point of view Plots to exact revenge	**Thoughts:** Does not overestimate the extent to which the other person acted deliberately Does not see malicious intent in the motives of others Does not see self as definitely right and the other person definitely wrong Able to see the other person's point of view Does not plot to exact revenge
Behaviours: To attack the other physically To attack the other verbally To attack the other passive-aggressively To displace the attack onto another person, an animal, or object To withdraw aggressively To recruit allies against the other	**Behaviours:** To assert self with the other To request, but not demand behavioural change from the other

Unhealthy	Healthy
Guilt	Remorse/Regret
Inference: Violation of moral code, failure to live up to moral code, hurts feelings of a significant other	
Thoughts: Assumes that one has definitely committed the sin Assumes more personal responsibility than the situation warrants Assigns far less responsibility to others than is warranted Does not think of mitigating factors Thinks that one will receive retribution	**Thoughts:** Considers behaviour in context and with understanding in making a final judgment concerning whether one has 'sinned' Assumes appropriate level of personal responsibility (not blame) Assigns appropriate level of responsibility to others Takes into account mitigating factors Does not think one will receive retribution
Behaviours: To escape from the unhealthy pain of guilt in self-defeating ways To beg for forgiveness from the person wronged To promise unrealistically that they will not sin again To punish self physically or by deprivation To disclaim responsibility for wrongdoing	**Behaviours:** To face up to the healthy pain that accompanies the realization that one has sinned To ask but not beg for forgiveness To understand reasons for wrongdoing and act on one's understanding To atone for the sin by taking a penalty To make appropriate amends No tendency to make excuses for one's behaviour or enact other defensive behaviour

Unhealthy	Healthy
Shame	Disappointment
Inference: Something shameful has been revealed about self (or group with whom one identifies) by self or others, others will look down or shun self (or group with whom one identifies)	
Thoughts: Overestimates the 'shamefulness' of the information revealed Overestimates the likelihood that the judging group will notice or be interested in the information Overestimates the degree of disapproval self (or reference group) will receive Overestimates the length of time any disapproval will last	**Thoughts:** See information revealed in a compassionate self-accepting context Is realistic about the likelihood that the judging group will notice or be interested in the information Is realistic about the degree of disapproval self (or reference group) will receive Is realistic about the length of time any disapproval will last
Behaviours: To remove self from the 'gaze' of others To isolate self from others To save face by attacking other(s) who have 'shamed' self To defend threatened self-esteem in self-defeating ways To ignore attempts by others to restore social equilibrium	**Behaviours:** To continue to participate actively in social interaction To respond to attempts of others to restore social equilibrium

Unhealthy	Healthy
Hurt	Sorrow
Inference: Other treats self badly (self undeserving)	
Thoughts: Underestimates the unfairness of the other person's behaviour Others perceived as showing lack of care or indifference Self seen as alone, uncared for, or misunderstood Tends to think of past 'hurts' Thinks that the other has to put things right of own accord first	**Thoughts:** Is realistic about the degree of unfairness of the other person's behaviour Others perceived as acting badly rather than as uncaring or indifferent Self not seen as alone, uncared for, or misunderstood Less likely to think of past hurts when hurt Doesn't think that the other has to make the first move
Behaviours: To shut down communication channel with the other To criticise the other without disclosing what one feels hurt about	**Behaviours:** To communicate one's feelings to the other directly To influence the other person to act in a fairer manner

Unhealthy	Healthy
Jealousy	Jealousy
Inference: Threat to relationship with a partner from another person	
Thoughts:	**Thoughts:**
Tends to see a threat to one's relationship when none really exists	Tends not to see threats to one's relationship when none exists
Thinks the loss of one's relationship is imminent	Does not misconstrue ordinary conversations between partner and other men/women
Misconstrues one's partners ordinary conversations as having romantic or sexual connotations	Does not construct visual images of partner's infidelity
Constructs visual images of partners infidelity	Accepts that partner will find other attractive but does not see this as a threat
If partner admits to finding another attractive, believes that the other is seen as more attractive than self and that one's partner will leave self for this other person	
Behaviours:	**Behaviours:**
To seek constant reassurance that one is loved	Tends not to see threats to one's relationship when none exists
To monitor the actions and feelings of one's partner	Does not misconstrue ordinary conversations between partner and other men/women
To search for evidence that one's partner is involved with someone else	Does not construct visual images of partner's infidelity
To attempt to restrict the movements or activities of one's partners	Accepts that partner will find other attractive but does not see this as a threat
To set tests which partner has to pass	
To retaliate for partner's presumed infidelity	
To sulk	

Unhealthy	Healthy
Envy	Envy
Inference: Another person possesses and enjoys something desirable that the person does not have	
Thoughts:	**Thoughts:**
Tends to denigrate the value of the desired possession	Honestly admits to oneself that one desires the desired possession
Tries to convince self that one is happy with one's possessions (although one is not)	Does not try to convince self that one is happy with one's possession when one is not
Thinks about how to acquire the desired possession regardless of its usefulness	Thinks about how to obtain the desired possession because one desires it for healthy reasons
Thinks about how to deprive the other person of the desired possession	Can allow the person to have and enjoy the desired possession without denigrating the person of the possession
Behaviours:	**Behaviours:**
To disparage verbally the person who has the desired possession	To obtain the desired possession if it is truly what one wants
To disparage verbally the desired possession	
To take away the desired possession from the other (either so that one will have it or the other will be deprived of it)	
To spoil or destroy the desired possession so that the other person does not have it.	

The above table provides not only an insight into the healthier version of the negative emotion and its counterpart but also clues as to how to respond, what you can control, to act in accordance with the healthier version. If you would like a copy of the table to download and work on, it can be downloaded at: **www.changeseminars.com/reclaim-handouts**. Also, you may like to try the QR code on the copyright page at the start of the book.

Anxiety vs Concern

Starting with Anxiety, if I haven't mentioned it already, I have a diagnosis of Generalised Anxiety Disorder. So, it's one that's close to home and prevalent for many. To be honest, if you've been through any military or basic training it may not be possible to finish, or if you were lucky enough to escape, without some experience of anxiety. For some it's simply for the time they are involved for others it can become a conditioned response.

There are of course many other triggers for anxiety, Psychology Today claims the following triggers: your health, prescription medication, caffeine, skipping meals, bills, taxes, and income loss, parties and social events, conflict, stress, public performances, and personal associations to name just a few.

How I've managed anxiety to date and how I continue to manage it through what we are discussing, replacing anxiety with concern requires deeper work which we'll go into. However, it's important to note that a thing called cognitive consequences is at play here, which impacts my anxiety. Understanding a threat to ourselves as the traditional view of anxiety holds, may be hard to define when we are in the zone of feeling anxious or experiencing anxiety. As helpful as the list above may be, it's characterized for me at least by overestimating the negative features of a situation and underestimating my ability to cope.

Often, just like how before this book you may have been unaware of the irrational beliefs that are being triggered when facing emotional upset, you can also be oblivious to the fact that you are underestimating your ability to cope. It's different for everyone, but for me underestimating my ability to cope was key and was manifesting through approaches such as I can't standititis as outlined earlier in terms of how beliefs manifest.

I'd explain it as overwhelm, feeling tapped out mentally, attempting to withdraw mentally and often physically. I'd often refer to the experience as whiting out. As if I closed my eyes and attempted to attributed a colour to it, the colour would be white. At the time whilst that was my indicator that I had tapped out, my attempt to escape my situation wasn't helping.

Just like yelling and screaming about your problems leads to an erroneous feeling of being in control, so whiting out made me think that it was helping. In fact, I was encouraging that behaviour and making it more of my go-to reaction. Just like the knee-jerk reaction of yelling and screaming about your problems it can start to feel like it controls or at least has a handle on you.

This is another example of avoidance behaviour and not taking action to work through and effectively manage my anxiety which is common. Whiting out really started to become an issue, when of all things I was discussing attending a surprise birthday party for a mate.

This was someone I did not want to let down, whilst discussing how I would attempt to get the family to come away for the weekend. Whiting out became my response and I realised I had to do something more about it. I have also had this become a problem years ago when finishing off my degree and on top of everything I had an aggressive over-the-top real estate agent to deal with, who treated tenants like the enemy.

If you look at the inference for unhealthy negative emotions in the table above, specifically with respect to anxiety. It identifies that in order for anxiety to exist, we view or infer the trigger as a threat or some form of danger. In the case of not wanting to let my mate down by attending the surprise party, the threat was letting that person down. I felt that I was in danger, somewhere in the far reaches of my mind, of having this occur. The irate real estate agent could have an impact on whether we had a roof over our heads and might influence our bond or tenancy record or something similar.

A way of viewing the threat realistically is to say, okay, this is a big deal. I'm feeling this way. Is it going to hurt me? One of the REBT approaches I took when I was working through some anxiety I had some time ago. I started the ABC approach to challenge myself around the anxiety and started to bring it back to concern.

And one of the questions I asked myself was, why am I trying to hurt myself? Because this response hurts. It's like a headache. For me. It's pressure. No doubt those of you who have anxiety feel similarly. I followed that question up with, where's the proof I need to feel this way? This is another classic REBT approach known as the scientific approach.

Why am I doing this

A great way to confront this is to ask yourself? The question of viewing the threat realistically is this threat, is whatever I'm getting stressed about, as dangerous as I'm telling myself? I mean no one's going to kill me. Is somebody chasing me down the road with an axe or a knife and trying to stab me? I had a mate once in the military who used to say when faced with the potential of breaking some overly oppressive military rule, 'What are they going to do, take a birthday off me?'

No of course not. It isn't a realistic threat, but appreciating what else may be occurring in your life, distracting you, or taxing your energy that may be affecting your capacity to cope. That's all part of acknowledging what is happening.

We can also use the same 5 point approach that we did for frustration.

1. Acknowledge your emotion (Anxiety in this case)
2. Analyse it through the ABC model
3. Immerse yourself in it (Through visualization)
4. Use your disputing skills to address it
5. Make it a habit

So above we've looked at how to acknowledge what is occurring, next we can view it through an ABC framework. In the example below I've put experiencing anxiety as the trigger as often it can be unclear as to the threat. This approach will also help if you are feeling secondary emotions about your anxiety, depression is one that can occur which does make it feel unclear as to what you are suffering from and even make anxiety feel like a trigger for depression or other emotions.

A. Activator: Identify your activator or trigger	B. Belief: (Circle all that apply)	C. Consequence: Identify your feelings and how you behave when triggered by this activator
Experiencing anxiety	(Self) Others Circumstances	**Feelings:** Stressed unable to cope, whiting out **Behaviour:** Withdraw psychologically and physically need to be on your own, engage in distracting behaviour need a drink, etc.

When I experience: Anxiety, I feel stressed and have an overwhelming desire to withdraw.

BECAUSE OF WHAT? Because I feel that I cannot cope, with transgressing my values or beliefs. That this might put me in a difficult situation that I am too busy to have to sort out.

My Belief, therefore, manifests as (Circle all that apply):

1. (Demanding)
2. (Catastrophising)
3. (I can't standititis)
4. Pejorative putdowns

Once this basic analysis is complete as shown above the next step is to immerse yourself into the anxiety. Given that there are no fairly innocuous activities we can do such as low frustration tolerance task, the best available approach for immersion is to revisit it via visualization.

In order to do this, simply find a comfortable place to sit, preferably where you won't be interrupted, close your eyes and take yourself back to when you experienced that anxiety. Where were you at the time? What was going on around you? Try to visualise it in as much detail as possible.

Next, if it feels safe to do so, remember self-care is the first and most important thing in this situation, imagine the anxiety levels increase. If it is an intensity level of 9 take it up to 10 or higher out of 10. Then imagine yourself reducing the anxiety, down below the score out of 10 you started with down to 7, 6 to 5, and think about what you are saying to yourself.

At some point see it stop being anxiety at all and start to enter the intensity level at about 5 or lower of concern. Start to feel that as the truth and your new reality. Once you open your eyes. Continue with step 4, work through disputing your anxiety.

D. Dispute:

1. **Is it true?** Is it true that I need to define what I am feeling as anxiety? Can I simply reclassify and re-lable what I am feeling as its healthy negative counterpart? I have just done so by use of visualization and see no reason why this is not the truth for how I am feeling in this moment.

2. **Does it logically follow?** Does it logically follow that my response to whatever the threat inference is, needs to be full blown anxiety? Of course not, concern is a more reasonable and supportive description in this situation and one that makes it easier to see the situation in a positive light.

3. **Is it helping?** Is it helping that I respond to whatever has triggered me as anxious? No, it only seeks to make me less able to function, and represents a bad choice that I can influence to become merely concerned.

> **E. Enforce your preferences:**
>
> Of course, I'd prefer that anxiety did not occur for me but that is currently how things are manifesting for me. I know it will not always be that way and that getting more upset or depressed about it isn't going to help. Taking proactive steps to reframe this response will help to alleviate follow-on emotions and hence my capacity for anxiety moving forward.

Lastly making it a habit by remembering to practice this approach when faced with your anxiety and practicing it a few times afterward, will help to instill the results and plan your response at a strategic level for your next stressful encounter.

Another technique that also helps particularly with anxiety is breathing. Dave Grossman author of 'On Killing' and the follow-up book 'On Combat', both of which I highly recommend, claimed that stopping and taking a sip of a bottle of water, forces you to change your breathing and slow it down when facing extreme anxiety and might help you get to a place where you can complete the 5 steps necessary to work through your anxiety. I've also come across a technique, though the source is unknown as the technique was passed to me 3rd hand. The claim is that anxiety cannot exist in a certain state that breathing in for 6 seconds and out again for 6 seconds can help you to achieve. The person who told me this has had great success not only with his own anxiety but with helping inmates in the corrections system. I recommend you give it a try.

One that I practice personally on a regular basis is box breathing, where you complete four steps at a count of four for each. Breathing in for four, holding for four, releasing for four, and holding once again for four and continuing that can be incredibly effective. I was introduced to a similar technique in the military and reminded of it recently on a Kinetic Fighting course. For more information on that course check out **https:// kineticfighting.com.au/**.

There are a few ways you can go about replacing the unhealthy version with the healthy version of an emotion and the ABC framework is a valuable tool for this. However, I wanted to share with you a shortcut to help you start implementing the healthy negative alternative straight away. It will not help you to complete the deeper work and may not work for all unhealthy negative emotions, but it has certainly helped me with anxiety.

When experiencing anxiety, I will often repeat the words 'Concern, Concern, Concern' in a firm tone. Indicating the healthy negative emotion that I am attempting to replace the unhealthy negative emotion with. This typically lowers the intensity of the experience and I can then make the call about whether this anxiety or whatever appears to be triggering it requires deeper work. Next, I ask the question, 'okay, what do I have to be concerned about?' When it's just something that might elicit an anxiety-based response, such as my kids screaming, I can easily diffuse the situation by accepting reality. If it's the kids, I'll just reply 'it's just the kids screaming, no big deal. Kids scream all the time and in this situation, it doesn't mean much.'

If it's something more important, I can commit to getting back to whatever the trigger is at a time that I can actually do the deeper work on the problem. When that occurs, I usually determine what action needs to be taken to address whatever is triggering me at that time.

Whilst this approach can be quite beneficial, completing an ABC process to work through the particular unhealthy negative emotion, as we have done previously is recommended. If not in the moment, at a convenient time later.

For the sake of demonstration and as you should already be across the process, let's look at our 3 questions for challenging your unhealthy negative emotion. In this instance, we would be focusing mostly on our emotions and not the circumstance as a whole.

In addition to working through the 5 step plan mentioned above and where you might not have the luxury to work through all 5 steps at one time. Try just disputing it in 3 steps, I have included different responses here as well:

1. **Is it true?** Is it true that what I am feeling is anxiety or would I be better served in labeling and hence attempting to achieve a level of concern when reflecting on how I feel about this situation, threat, or trigger?
2. **Does it logically follow?** Does it logically follow that I need to go to the extreme unhealthy negative emotion in this instance or would it be easier to deal with at the level of concern? Would it also follow the same level of logic to be concerned when facing this type of threat in the future?
3. **Is it helping?** It's clearly not helping as acceptance of this extremely unhealthy negative emotion is quite debilitating and I have things to deal with and other demands that require my attention.

Even the process of choosing, well let's face it, it's more insisting with yourself that you are going to lable what you are feeling as the healthy version of the negative emotion, not accepting your negative self-talk, deviating from that negative definition may be what is required. Making the leap of faith to this approach and committing to it as close to 100% as you can will certainly help.

Where the healthy version is simply titled healthy then the name of the emotion, as in the case of anger, simply attempting to label your emotions as healthy anger might make this habit a little ambiguous. You might define how you are feeling as mad, or livid, but it's worth looking into the behaviours and thoughts of that emotion and using those as ways to check your responses and give you habits to practice. As you may have already determined this does require a fair degree of introspection.

In the case of anger ask:

Am I overestimating the extent to which the other person acted deliberately?

Do I believe that malicious intent is motivating those involved?

Do I see myself as definitely right, and others involved as definitely wrong?

Can I see it from the other person's point of view?

Have I considered what that might be?

Have I plotted to exact revenge?

Using these questions should help to elicit asking the 3 questions to dispute, it may also make you aware of what you are actually doing. Those questions again are: Is it true? Does it logically follow? Is it helping?

Replacing unhealthy negative emotions with healthy negative emotions may take some work, so be prepared for the challenge. You may be working against a lifetime of conditioning, so be patient, it will come and perhaps faster than you think. You may also benefit, from being proactive regarding your emotions. Use some introspection and reflect on a time in your life when you experienced any of the unhealthy negative emotions, or multiple times if it has become a bad habit to respond that way. Remember we can't change the past, only how we feel about the past. This approach can be quite cathartic.

CHAPTER 9

DEALING WITH SHAME

> 'Shame is nothing more than denial of the truth.'
> —M. FUNKHOUSER

As we've seen in the previous chapter, shame is an unhealthy negative emotion and its healthy counterpart is disappointment. Shame and embarrassment are similar and often confused, however, they differ in the fact that shame is caused by an individual act often known to oneself and embarrassment is an emotion assigned to an act that is deemed not socially fitting.

If we look at the thought patterns of someone experiencing shame outlined in the previous chapter they include:

- Overestimates the 'shamefulness' of the information revealed
- Overestimates the likelihood that the judging group will notice or be interested in the information
- Overestimates the degree of social disapproval self (or reference group) will receive
- Overestimates the length of time any disapproval will last

Notice that all of these thoughts involve overestimating, therefore it would follow that overreacting is also required. Achieving disappointment requires:

- That you see information revealed in a compassionate self-accepting context
- Is realistic about the likelihood that the judging group will notice or be interested in the information
- Is realistic about the degree of disapproval self (or reference group) will receive
- Is realistic about the length of time any disapproval will last

Some of the tools already discussed throughout the book include accepting oneself unconditionally, circles of control, and the ABC model. Unconditional self-acceptance requires forgiveness and this can be a powerful tool in dealing with shame. There is more to the puzzle of working through shame as it does have some unique characteristics and opens itself up to an important immersion tactic which will be discussed further.

Many men deal with shame, hence its inclusion in this book as simply telling someone not to 'give a shit' really doesn't cut it. Although you may have been given such advice in the past.

Understanding where shame comes from involves understanding the difference between events and inferences. Events are something that you can prove occurred, inferences on the other hand are an attempt to describe what happened. But as an inference, it is not fact and needs to be tested against reality or at the very least other people's recollection of events.

Maintenance of shame relies heavily on accepting inference as fact and not testing it against reality. Inferences include the overestimation of the facts mentioned above. Even if inferences can be supported, they may only be true in part and where a person finds themselves feeling a sense of shame that a social group may not accept them as a result, it's impossible to account for the opinions of all members of the group.

Remember when we were looking at emotional reasoning in the unhelpful patterns of thinking (cognitive distortions). The belief that if you feel it, it must be true supports the belief in shame very well. As part of moving past a shameful existence, accepting oneself and instead choosing to back yourself, to live on purpose is an important step. This will help you to feel at worst mild disappointment when someone finds out some deep dark secret that you'd prefer not to be made public. Choosing to own your space is also useful as is being assertive.

Shame is a socially motivated emotion. It occurs when in the presence of others, or when you have others at the forefront of your mind, when alone, reflecting on something that occurred.

Research shows that we can feel ashamed when we fall short of our ideals. Triggers of shame can also include; behaviors, thoughts and images, body blemishes, and deformities.

For people to feel ashamed, either by letting down a reference group or being let down by a member of a reference group this can occur, particularly if you feel an affiliation or affinity with that group. Being exposed to the judgment of others is also a common trigger for shame. The threat of appearing vulnerable in public is a trigger for a lot of men, however, overcoming this fear is a very important step.

Why? Because it shows you're human, it's a leadership trait as it helps others to realise it's ok to show emotion. Just imagine you are catching up with mates at a bar. Someone brings along a new friend, someone you haven't met yet. For some reason in the telling of a story in the course of conversation, you share something that leads you to get emotional. Who knows, perhaps you are worried about one of your kids, or perhaps you just lost a job or anything that might trigger you.

If you are able to do so without trying to hide it, you will influence others to realise it's okay, you may even help this new guy to think it's okay too. It might help him to show emotion where perhaps he hadn't previously and possibly even prevent him from going too far when things get tough. You never know how far this level of influence could stretch.

Unfortunately, guys feel that they have to be what society today deems as stoic in the face of emotions. The term today is used to mean not showing emotion, however, the Stoics believed in showing emotion and acknowledged the presence of emotion. Robertson (2020).

An important distinction needs to be drawn between believing an event caused shame and identifying an event that led people to feel shame. This distinction will help you to overcome your shame. If you look at the two phrases, one indicates a belief that implies shame is inevitable and you cannot escape the event without being impacted by it. The other implies you have made a choice. This reflects what was discussed in the introduction, that everything is a choice, and the quote by Epictetus earlier in the book that

'Men are disturbed, not by things but by the view which they take of them.'

To follow with a basic ABC model to illustrate this, from the anecdote above about you showing emotion in front of mates at the pub. In the table below we are going to take a slightly different approach to viewing our emotional upset with respect to shame.

| A. Activator: Identify your activator or trigger Showing emotion in front of mates at the pub | B. Belief: (Circle all that apply) ⦿Self⦿ ⦿Others⦿ Circumstances I must not show emotion in front of mates at the pub (Demand) | C. Consequence: Identify your feelings and behaviours when triggered by this activator **Feelings:** Shame, feel the need to leave **Behaviour:** leave the gathering early claiming to not be feeling well |

Showing emotion in front of mates at the pub	I would prefer not to show emotion in front of mates at the pub **(preference)**	**Feelings:** Disappointment **Behaviour:** Try to stop showing emotion as quickly as possible
Showing emotion in front of mates at the pub	I don't really care either way if I show emotion in front of mates at the pub. **(indifference)**	**Feelings:** Okay, no emotional upset, or ill feelings toward self **Behaviour:** Continue evening as normal

As you can see above, we have compared, a demand about yourself with respect to showing emotion in public. The demand holds that you absolutely must not show emotion in public. A more desirable approach is to reduce your demand to a preference, with the ultimate outcome being indifference.

As you can see demand is at the center of our feelings about shame, it is termed irrational in REBT as it is a rigid belief, inconsistent with reality, it is illogical, and produces unhelpful behavioural and emotional outcomes Dryden (1997).

You may recall the way in which irrational beliefs manifested previously in the book as being demands, awfulizing, I can't standititis, and pejorative putdowns. Depending on who you are reading from, in an REBT textbook, the way beliefs manifest can also be called beliefs themselves. This is confusing, however, for the sake of clarity we will bring them under the belief about self, as shame requires us to focus on ourselves often erroneously for an excessive amount of time.

In addition to our rigidly held or irrational beliefs, shame also invokes self-depreciation of which there are 3 versions. These could be classified as pejorative putdowns about the self, beliefs of self-depreciation are quite prevalent in the experience of shame. It is however important to be aware that you will at some stage in the shame game experience it. Especially if you find, when exploring your shame behaviours and emotions you find it unclear as to exactly which belief you are experiencing, or if it appears to be more than just a belief about self as you currently understand it.

The thing to remember is that shame is a socially based emotion, given that in caveman days societal approval was important to survival, these feelings can run deep. When engaging in self-depreciation, you may feel as if you are one of three things:

1. The diminished self
2. The defective self
3. The socially repellant self

In the diminished self you may say that you feel small or insignificant, whilst not emotions, what these descriptions indicate is that when experiencing shame, you can experience yourself as diminished or less than. Your feelings of shame may be followed by feelings of powerlessness, viewing others as more powerful. You may see these big powerful others, as you may have created them in your mind, as potentially likely to exercise their power over you for whatever shameful act you may have committed, or at least believed you have committed.

You may experience these others as a cause of ridicule or another attitude that may indicate they are looking down upon you. Not always based in fact. This feeling of being looked down upon is common in this form of self-depreciation. An example of this might be in the case of showing emotions in front of mates at the pub, if they don't act in a way that appears supportive straight away, as many men take time to respond or let things sink in, you may erroneously interpret their behaviour as looking down upon you. Some of those present may not attend the next social gathering which could potentially play further on your mind as the sense of diminished self if you are hanging on their response.

The defective self requires you to view yourself as defective and to be ashamed of that. This occurs most often when you reveal a part of yourself as broken or defective, to a social group. This can be a defect that exists or that you feel exists and gains traction if you tend to view others in the desired social group as being without defect or flaw entirely. You may wonder what they see in someone as defective as you, and why they would want to associate with yourself.

I certainly experienced this as a kid, with a feeling of being uncoordinated, something which I processed through skateboarding as an individual pursuit. I couldn't run too fast or kick a ball well enough and never felt as though I fit in with team sports. I'd counter the feelings instead of letting them manifest into shame or embarrassment. I can freely recall determining never to buy into shame in my late teens whilst experiencing bullying.

Today I take ownership of this sort of thing, freely admitting that I was never the most natural soldier, throughout my army career. Instead committing myself to the 'long haul' approach of being what I like to think of as a work in progress. Focusing on what I am good at in the people space and getting satisfaction from that, is a way I have been able to concern myself less with what could potentially be a source of shame if I let it become that.

The Defective Self may manifest in showing emotion in front of mates at the pub and you see yourself as defective, unable to keep it together in front of others. As if everyone all of the time must keep it together.

The socially repellent self, not unlike how you may think someone like the elephant man might be viewed or the untouchables in India might feel. This type of shame can occur for people with obvious deformities or body blemishes, people who have been sexually abused can also experience this. It's important to note that similar to the irrational beliefs of self, others, and circumstance, you might be experiencing more than one of them at the same time. When attempting to work through feelings of shame determine which type of self-depreciation you are going to work on at the time, instead of attempting to solve everything at once.

In additional ways in which they manifest, you may recall awfulizing, but frustration can also play a part. Whilst unmet demands and self-depreciation are considered primary determinants of shame, low frustration tolerance which we discussed earlier and awfulizing previously discussed as to how beliefs manifest can affect this.

Awfulising in the role shame takes involves as the name suggests, believing that it is 100% bad that you have committed a shameful act or that nothing could be worse than whatever it was you did in the first place. Let's say you revealed a weakness, or what you consider to be a weakness, by being vulnerable in front of mates at the pub. You may awfulize that this is the worst thing that you could do.

Low frustration tolerance comes into play when you believe that you cannot handle the fact that you were vulnerable, you will literally cease to exist if the event continues to unfold or you will forfeit any future happiness as a result. This is of course not true, but it is still what we can tell ourselves when playing the shame game, and are all important to be aware of.

Check-In

If you wrestle with shame, think back to something that caused you to be ashamed in light of the information in this chapter. Stop and reflect for a few minutes.

Ask:

- Do you tend to overestimate elements of the shame mentioned earlier in the chapter?
- Are you making demands about the act that led you to feel shame?
- Have you experienced self-depreciation as a result?

If so which of the 3 ways, have you done this? (Circle all that apply)

- The diminished self
- The defective self
- The socially repellant self

Do you engage in awfulizing or low frustration tolerance?

Have you applied the lessons of the chapter on frustration to this situation?

Behaviours we perform when experiencing shame are important to note, as you may well be performing them and not be aware that you in fact may be experiencing a type of shame. The behaviours as listed in the chapter on unhealthy negative emotions are:

- To remove self from the 'gaze' of others
- To isolate self from others
- To save face by attacking other(s) who have 'shamed' self
- To defend threatened self-esteem in self-defeating ways
- To ignore attempts by others to restore social equilibrium

These behaviours can also be considered action tendencies which are in effect, how you would prefer to act when confronted with something that triggers you to feel shame. Removing yourself from the gaze of others or averting your eyes from them allows you to partially withdraw from others. You may not be able to withdraw from others but this may be considered the next best thing.

If we consider all of the above behaviours in the context of showing emotion in front of mates at the pub you could do all 5 quite easily. Your action tendency may be to physically withdraw, but the 'accepted' behaviour is to not return the eye contact of others.

You may isolate yourself from future contact with the group with whom you were at the pub, avoiding attending social gatherings with them even for a period of time. If someone looks at all uncomfortable with your display of emotion, you might have a joke at their expense about something unrelated afterward in front of everyone.

You may refuse attempts of members of the group who reach out to comfort you and you might attempt self-defeating behaviours such as drinking more than you might otherwise. All of these behaviours do not help. So, what does?

Well, let's begin by examining our healthy alternative to shame, disappointment. Disappointment works as a healthy alternative to shame for many reasons but the two I will mention here are that you can feel disappointed about the same things that you feel shame about. You can feel disappointed about something without the self-depreciation that is at the core of shame. Lastly, it serves as a healthy alternative as you do not need to defend yourself against it.

Shame allows us to work similarly to how we operated with frustration in that we can use our 5 point plan from before.

1. Identify a situation in your past that you felt ashamed of and acknowledge the shame.
2. Analyse through the ABC lens.

A. Activator: Identify your activator or trigger Showing emotion in front of mates at the pub	B. Belief: (Circle all that apply) (Self) (Others) Circumstances I must not show emotion in front of mates at the pub (Demand)	C. Consequence: Identify your feelings and how you behave when triggered by this activator Feelings: Shame, feel the need to leave Behaviour: Leave the gathering early claiming to not be feeling well

When: I showed emotion in front of mates in the pub

I felt: Deeply Ashamed, uncomfortable, I felt the need to leave. I did not want to be there. I felt less than myself, diminished somehow even defective

And Behaved: In an awkward manner, not making eye contact and resisting attempts by mates to comfort me or acknowledge support from my friends. I felt the need to drink more

BECAUSE OF WHAT? Because I should be able to keep it together and not show emotion when I don't think it is appropriate or necessary.

My Belief, therefore, manifests as (Circle all that apply):
1. (Demanding)
2. (Catastrophising)
3. I can't standititis
4. (Pejorative putdowns)

3. At this stage we need to immerse ourselves in shame, you may use rational emotive imagery again here, however, REBT provides an immersion approach that is unique to being ashamed. Do something embarrassing! That's right,

the technical term is a 'shame attack exercise' and can involve doing anything in public that you might find shameful or embarrassing. You could choose something specific to whatever you are feeling ashamed of currently, but you might struggle to start crying in front of mates at a pub if that was what you had chosen to upset yourself about. In my 10 module online program of the same name as this book, I videoed myself skipping up and down High Street, Penrith, and attempting to sing, which I found quite liberating. A client of mine once stripped down to his boxer shorts and walked around his local park with an umbrella. Whatever it is, if you can't make it the same thing as what you are ashamed about, be mindful of your shame whilst you complete the exercise.

Other examples include:

- Riding a train or bus and announcing the stations as they come out as loudly as you can
- Reading aloud from a children's book on a train or bus is also a good one
- Put a bag over your head on a bus or train or even in a public place where you can sit and be noticed
- Tow a banana on a string down a busy street
- Lie on the ground for 30 seconds in a public place and then get up, smile, and pretend nothing has happened or invite others to join you

The above examples were from https://feelinggood.com/wp-content/uploads/2019/ 01/Shame-Attackng-v-1.pdf there are plenty more online a simple search for shame attack will bring up many more.

A word of advice, with shame attacking exercises, do not do anything that is illegal, immoral, likely to cause harm to others or yourself, cause you to lose your job or your friendships. What you will find however is that once you have had regular practice of REBT techniques and can use them to great effect, completing a shame attack exercise will help you to make the use of the ABC model and the techniques involved, a lot closer to being automatic. You might even find the experience liberating.

4. Next, once you have confronted your shame or shame in general dependent on the specificity of your shame attack exercise, disputing what you are ashamed of will now feel easier. See the table below for guidance on our showing emotions in the pub scenario mentioned throughout the chapter.

> **D. Dispute:**
>
> 1. **Is it true?** Is it true that I have committed a shameful act? Certainly not, we all show emotion from time to time, perhaps I'm just not comfortable doing so in the pub over beers with mates. It's also not true that I am any less of a person for showing emotion, and that feeling shame is not necessarily the only possible outcome.
>
> 2. **Does it logically follow?** It does not logically follow that I need to feel embarrassed or shameful in response to showing emotion. At that moment I may have made it okay for others in the group to do likewise. It doesn't logically follow that at that moment I am any less of a person, or somehow defective. I did, before my social conditioning kicked in triggering embarrassment, actually feel relief even for a brief moment.
>
> 3. **Is it helping?** It certainly is not helping to feel this way, the feeling of shame leads me to want to shut down and not talk to anyone, to hide away from the world, hoping it will all go away. As an adult taking ownership of my emotions means I have nothing to hide and if others think less of me that's their problem.

> **E. Enforce your preferences:**
> Of course, I have had a preference and at times a demand that I not feel this way or act this way in public, but life doesn't work that way and if I am to live in accordance with reality, I need to think differently about how I show or don't show emotions.

5. Finally making confronting your shame a habit is important especially if you are still holding on to past shame or have a history of experiencing it. Regular shame attack exercises even by themselves can be a great start.

As you can see above, deciding to confront how you feel about your shame does not have to be difficult or scary, and we are making it that way for ourselves by choosing to go along with old habits and beliefs about shame. Owning the problem and taking responsibility for our shame does not need to be some bold approach where you need to act aggressively toward your feelings. As you may have already started to accept, whilst this approach that is used throughout the book requires taking responsibility for your emotions, it is a world away from blame.

Unconditional Self-Acceptance also plays a role in dealing with shame, most notably in better understanding disappointment. You may so far have noticed that each of the main tenants of REBT pop up again, either consistently in terms of what we tend to focus on, or at other points throughout the various emotions and how we deal with them.

Note that in order to feel ashamed you need to rate yourself, whilst I jokingly referred to my father's definition of the self earlier in the book, a reasonable version can be found in Hauck (1991). The author Paul Hauck, claims the self is 'every conceivable thing about you that can be rated'. With this definition, it's easy to see how we can either choose to or not to rate the self.

If you consider that everything that has ever happened to you or ever will happen to you in your entire life, it's impossible to believe that you can accurately rate the self. If we consider unconditional self-acceptance in the context of showing emotions in front of mates at the pub, it may reasonably follow that you consider your behaviour to be undesirable or weak, but not yourself. Taking into account the chapter on Unconditional Self-Acceptance requiring a refusal to rate the self as anything other than a fallible worthwhile human being Dryden (1997).

Therefore, if you consider your display of emotion to be weak or less than preferable, do not overgeneralise those feelings to an erroneous rating system of yourself. Instead of viewing yourself as a participant in this situation, that for you that behaviour was not okay. It's far easier to work on responding differently if that is your choice when these sorts of feelings come up in public.

If you consider unconditional self-acceptance as an option, it's likely that shame will not be possible or at least difficult to achieve for you. Shame as we have already discussed requires a rating of the self. If need be, go back to our exercise from chapter 4 hold your hand in front of your nose and mouth a few centimeters away, and wait, if the first thing you notice is that you can breathe, relax that's all you need.

I personally do not believe that it is weak to show emotion in public as indicated previously, it's up to you and you can choose to be okay with it or not. Ensuring you are okay, makes dealing with it as being good or bad as your preferences may dictate is up to you. My view on expressing the natural emotion of sadness, if it presents in such a way that you can display it, stems from accepting reality and seeing it as a strength that can influence others. It's also a great pressure release, and whilst we can release pressure in other ways a good cry is never a bad thing.

CHAPTER 10

OPERATIONALISING YOUR VALUES

'If you don't stick to your values when they are being tested, they're not values, they're hobbies'

—JON STEWART

In this chapter, we are going to visit values, help to rediscover what they are, possibly chose some new ones, and learn how to use those values as inspiration when things get too difficult. Values are something that can change but not that often, just like the rating of yourself as a fallible worthwhile human being. Your values don't go up or down and choosing to live in accordance with them can give you consistency when all around seems to be going crazy. Given what is going on in the world today that's something we all need.

If you consider everything that we have covered so far and if you have been actively participating in the activities and doing the work on yourself you will by now have a reasonable set of skills. You will also have a reasonable capacity to be able to apply what you have learned. Practice will only increase this, however, what I believe will invigorate the whole process for you is values. The reason why I have put it at the end is if you have been taking action, you will be able to make more out of getting clear about your values.

Values also help us to work within our circle of control and to achieve what I mentioned at the start of the book. To be able to reduce our circle of concern down to our circle of control, values are a vital part. Perhaps for achieving that outcome with what I have shared, this is the last piece of the puzzle.

Just like philosophy, you have values whether you realise it or not. By choosing or identifying what they are or what you would prefer them to be and adhering to them, you can begin to transform who you are and what you can achieve.

When I was in the army the values were courage, initiative and teamwork, which were extended to include respect, which I think has always been part of the military but it certainly was worth adding.

In order to make values relevant today, and why you should care about them, occurs if we operationalise them, hence the name of this chapter. By operationalising them I mean to actually live in accordance with them, to revisit them, and to ensure our actions are consistent with them. Many large organisations, talk about their values only at key times almost like a sales pitch. Using the military as an example again, I've heard leaders mention values as a way of puffing out a speech or a eulogy. They might say something like 'he was the embodiment of army values' or something similar.

You'll remember strategic vs tactical form earlier in the book, it's a process that I often share with my audiences to help them grasp the concept of operationalising. Strategic requires as you'd expect making decisions and plans to do something. For most people when it comes to values that's often where they stop. Decide on them and off you go, perhaps to be revisited somewhere in the future. Tactical on the other hand is like boots on the ground, the difference between that and being strategic is easily explained with a military analogy. Strategic is the officers and senior non-commissioned officers planning an operation, tactical is what the teams actually do on the ground.

Determining your values is strategic, how you live by them requires effort in the tactical space, or the real world to be more accurate.

One of the best examples I have come across for making values tactical is with the research done on willpower and self-control. In the book 'The Willpower Instinct' by Kelly McGonigal, she uses a unique way to describe how your values can help you to achieve whatever you need to get done.

Will Power Model

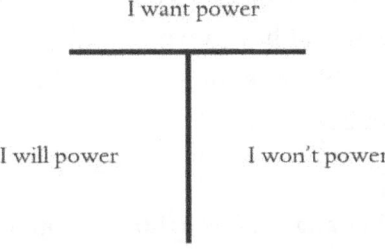

In the above diagram once again working within the limitations of Microsoft Word, the bottom section illustrates willpower for example, from the point of view of attempting to give something up. Each of the statements in the diagram represents a way of illustrating the elements of willpower and self-control. Let's say it's overeating and losing weight is what you are trying to achieve. I will power might pertain to, I will exercise and eat healthily, I won't power might pertain to, I won't sit on the couch for hours and eat unhealthy food.

These are great ideas and have their merit, however, that is usually as far as most people get. When motivation wanes, they go back to their old habits and either give up entirely or beat themselves up for failing at their attempt. Labeling themselves a failure as we know is incredibly hard to come back from and leaves people feeling lost and that it's all too hard.

Where the statement, I want power comes in is at that point where motivation wanes and we feel like giving up. I want power means that I want to be that person who lives by whichever values I have identified will help me to lose weight and get healthy.

Some values that come to mind if you are trying to achieve the above outcome might be discipline, toughness, and consistency. When you feel unmotivated to use the I want power approach ask how would someone who is disciplined act?

Your response might be, 'well I'm hungry, bored of the healthy food, haven't lost much weight this week. I feel like quitting, it's all too hard.' A disciplined person would have a workout, try for one more push-up, chin-up, or squat, possibly look for a new healthy alternative food-wise that tasted different or better than chicken rice and broccoli (insert bland diet in here).

They might realise that engaging toughness, would require them to put up with the feelings of wanting to quit. Phrases like 'This is why I am doing this' come to mind, they might challenge themselves through an ABC model and forgive themselves for having these feelings and understanding that if they do fall off, they can get back on tomorrow. Using consistency would mean similarly to discipline that they need to keep putting in every day and that results don't always come when you want them to.

Accompanying this approach is moving away from rigid attitudes or beliefs about what it is you are trying to achieve. Being flexible in our approach believe it or not is actually more effective. Often, we are told if we want to achieve something we need to be dogged in our determination and not waiver from that attitude to achieve whatever it is. However, a rigid approach can lead us to accept nothing less, this then leaves us no room for overcoming obstacles, and overgeneralising and judging ourselves as failures when things don't work out is also part of a rigid pattern of thinking.

Instead, if we would like to lose weight, or get down to a specific weight, or get up to a specific weight if you are a bodybuilder or serious weight lifter, you would be better served by holding the view that 'I would very much prefer to achieve a weight of X number of kilos or pounds and will do everything I can to achieve that. However, if I do not it is not the end of the world and I accept myself regardless.' It's important to note that, by claiming this I am not saying, I really want to or I must achieve X weight but it's ok if I don't and give up. That's a black and white or dichotomous approach and I am asking you to be flexible and to work within the grey areas.

If you are used to demanding that you must achieve your outcomes and anything less is a failure, you may achieve what it is that you are aiming at but fail to enjoy the process. Remember life is a journey not always a destination.

I used weight loss in the above example as it includes a lot of mental health elements and many people, men included, struggle with it. It's also a common goal to improve your physical state, whether you want to lose weight, drop body fat or get fitter.

One of the most important points to engaging your values is that the 'I want power' approach puts your values into action. A way to get you started down this path once you have settled on your values is to ask, what do these values mean to me? How am I going to put them into action?

One of the best ways to choose them that I have come across came from a book called The Program, by Eric Kapitulik. In it, he describes a timed approach to determining your values. It's the timed approach that applies pressure to your decision process that helps you to make decisions based on what you truly believe and in the case of values who or what you want to align with.

Values activity.

Step one: I have included is a list of 64 potential core values. For this step. I want you to take five minutes and break down your top 10 out of the 64. Remember to time yourself.

Step two: Now time 60 seconds. Break that 10 down to five. Put yourself under some pressure here because what will come out will be a determinant of your core values, your core values are an indication of the basis of who you are, these come out when you're under pressure.

Step three: Once you have five, take 10 seconds. Break that five up to three or four. Those 3 or 4 should be your core values. Now, that might be merely revisiting what you already have chosen in the past or in some other program, and that's fine. It might be confirmation of who you are. Hopefully, you have come away with something new, this may be the first time you have tried this and have learned something about yourself.

Even if you've done this stuff before, have a go again, revisit your core values. They're not supposed to change that much, but they may have altered or changed slightly since the last time you did an exercise like this. That's why I gave you a list of 64.

That's not a definitive list. There might be hundreds. If you have another list that you like as well, feel free to use that. Just use a list. Take a few minutes.

Step four: choose three or four. The purpose of three or four, take a few minutes to consider whether it should be three, whether it should be four.

We're giving you some leeway here. It doesn't have to be three or four. It'll be one or the other for you. Have that conversation with yourself and determine which will be best for you. Then, as you're setting those rules for yourself and you understand what that is, think of all the things we've covered so far.

Have you developed new values having seen how things work in managing your emotions and mental health?

Core Values List

Authenticity	Authority	Adventure	Achievement
Autonomy	Balance	Beauty	Boldness
Compassion	Challenge	Citizenship	Community
Competency	Curiosity	Creativity	Contribution
Fallibility	Fairness	Faith	Determination
Friendship	Fun	Growth	Happiness
Honesty	Humour	Influence	Inner Harmony
Justice	Kindness	Knowledge	Leadership
Learning	Love	Loyalty	Meaningful work
Openness	Optimism	Peace	Pleasure
Popularity	Poise	Religion	Recognition
Reputation	Respect	Security	Responsibility
Self Respect	Service	Success	Spirituality
Status	Wisdom	Wealth	Trustworthiness
Toughness	Discipline	Punctuality	Selflessness
Teamwork	Flexibility	Self Control	Self-Acceptance

Well, we couldn't leave you with that because it just gets you to the start point, to the first point of discovering what your values are. What you do with those values is perhaps more important than knowing what they are. What good are values that you think about once then ignore and go back to being who you were before and never revisit them again?

To finish up the section on values and the book itself, I'll share with you how I operationalise my values, what they are and how I prioritise them. The reason I haven't mentioned them until now is that I did not want to influence your choice of values. My core values are Toughness Teamwork and Self Discipline. There are more however these are my core values.

I'll start with Teamwork, the way that I operationalise this is in a few ways, the first is communication. If you have done the first exercise the next thing is to decide on a word or a few words that define that value for you. One word is best but may not be possible. Whatever you come up with it needs to be short and digestible.

The next one is toughness, I used to define this as pushing through what you don't want to do to get where you have to be. However, after learning from Kapitulik & MacDonald (2019), I prefer their definition: 'Doing what's right, not what's easy.' Now right isn't always clear and sometimes can turn out to be wrong, but often the easy way isn't the right way. I'll ask myself am I doing this because it's easy? When faced with a challenge, or is there a better way to do it? One that might be harder, that's okay. However, I'd like to share that I don't do something the hard way just because it is difficult either as that wouldn't make sense.

The third is Self Discipline, after Teamwork this is probably the one, I use the most. I've already mentioned 'discipline equals freedom' by Jocko Willink, Willink (2020). Part of the reason I joined the military in my 20's was to develop discipline. Too much discipline is not a good thing and it's important you get the right amount for yourself, but enough discipline can be liberating. A lot of people look at the concept of discipline as the unappealing part of the military, or someone yelling at them. There is a big difference between regimental discipline and self-discipline. Discipline is vital to be able to stick to achieving anything, without it you can wander of course, and fall back into old patterns that don't serve you.

I was often told that I was the most nonarmy person at work when I served, which I took as a compliment. You might be, or know someone who served. Sometimes my friends who served are meticulously clean around the home. Personally, I hate cleaning, however, I love self-discipline, so that has helped me to overcome how much I don't enjoy housework. Using REBT requires discipline, but just like our mate Jocko claims 'you want freedom you need to apply the discipline.' Finally, for me, discipline means doing what I say I will do and sticking to it, following through. Meeting my weekly goals of physical training, modifying that training to be able to complete obstacle races or whatever physical challenges I set for myself. Sticking to a rational approach when faced with adversity. What are yours?

To further operationalise my values I also use a priority approach to achieving anything. You may have heard this one, it's fairly simple: Mission first, Team second, Individual third. The individual is more often than not me. If I am working on a project team, or trying to achieve anything I tend to use this approach as it reminds me on a daily basis what's important.

In my family, the mission changes often depending on what we are doing, but the overall mission remains. To raise 3 happy, healthy, well-adjusted kids. To do this my wife and I are the team, my needs come last which is fine with me. Prior to having kids, I spent too much time focusing on myself, and a driving factor for having a family was to give myself entirely to them. That's not to say I neglect my needs but I tend to them once my support of my wife and kids are met.

I often come across self-improvement groups and practitioners, who insist it must be you that is most important in your life. That to me is too ego-focused and too rolled up in self-esteem. I believe, Self Esteem, Ego and Self Worth are the trio of self-deception. If you put yourself first that's fine, no disrespect to your choice. By putting my family first, it doesn't mean I necessarily do it at the expense of my needs, it's just that I can take care of myself with much less effort and in a much shorter space of time than my family requires. Looking after and caring for them meets many of my needs.

When working on a project team, obviously delivering the project outcomes come first. As a change manager, my client's needs and working to minimise the impact to them as a result of whatever I am delivering becomes paramount. My team and supporting them come second. If I put the team first when people left the workgroup, things could come unstuck fairly easily as getting on with the mission would be compromised. I am generally getting what I need so coming third is easy. Ensuring your needs get met, can include many things. I take time to ensure I get enough exercise, but also a regular massage and I see a counselor every two weeks. It allows me to work through any anxieties and keep my mind sharp.

When reflecting on how you are aligning to your values, determine an action that you can complete that keeps you aligned, is it prioritising as I've mentioned? Ask yourself as you reflect, have I met or been aligned to my values today? Determine easy-to-implement practices and disciplines to achieve this.

You have now reached the end of this book, thank you for getting this far. I hope the concepts and my system are of benefit, please let me know how it has worked for you, by visiting my Facebook group the Men's Mental Health Transformation. I know if you implement my system and these strategies, it will change your life, just as it has mine.

If I could leave you with one quote that sums up my approach it would be this, from the 80's skate rock band the Descendents, the song Coolidge from the Album All, that I used to listen to. I feel this quote is important for maintaining or finding the drive to keep going and might help you find some comfort when things get tough.

It certainly helps me strategically, how you make it work tactically is up to you.

'I looked up one day and saw that it was up to me, you can only be a victim if you admit defeat...'

Karl Alvarez

FURTHER READING

de Becker, G. (1998), *The Gift of Fear: And Other Survival Skills That Protect Us from Violence.* Dell.

Ellis, A. (2005), *The Myth of Self Esteem: How Rational Emotive Behaviour Therapy Can Change Your Life Forever.* Prometheus Books. New York.

Fryer, D. (2019), *The Four Thoughts That F*ck You Up, and how to fix them.* Penguin Random House. London.

Goggins, D. (2018). *Can't Hurt Me: Master Your Mind and Defy the Odds.* Lion Crest Publishing - Audible version advised

McGonigal, K. (2013), *The Willpower Instinct: How Self-Control Works, Why It Matters, and What You Can Do to Get More of It.* Avery Publishing.

Robertson, D. (2020), *How to Think Like a Roman Emperor,* The Stoic Philosophy of Marcus Aurelius. St Martin's Griffith. New York.

REFERENCES

Ellis, A. (2019), *How to Control Your Anxiety: Before it Controls You.* Robinson. United Kingdom.

Fryer, D. (2019), *The Four Thoughts That F*ck You Up,* and how to fix them. Penguin Random House. London.

Dryden, W. (1999) *Rational Emotive Behaviour Therapy: A Training Manual.* Springer Publishing

Dryden, W. (1997), *Overcoming Shame.* Sheldon Press. London.

Kapitulik, E. & MacDonald, J. (2019), The Program: Lessons from Elite Military Units for Creating and Sustaining High Performance Leaders and Teams. Wiley

McGonigal, K. (2013), *The Willpower Instinct: How Self-Control Works, Why It Matters, and What You Can Do to Get More of It.* Avery Publishing.

Miller, T. (1986), *The Unfair Advantage.* Lakeside Printing. New York.

Robertson, D. (2020), *How to Think Like a Roman Emperor,* The Stoic Philosophy of Marcus Aurelius. St Martin's Griffith. New York.

Hauck, P. (1991), *Hold Your Head Up High.* Sheldon Press. London

Willink, J. & Babin, L. (2018), *Extreme Ownership: How Navy Seals Lead and Win.* Macmillan. Australia

Willink, J. (2020), *Discipline Equals Freedom Field Manual MK1-Mod1 Expanded Edition.* St. Martin's Press. New York.

www.ingramcontent.com/pod-product-compliance
Lightning Source LLC
Chambersburg PA
CBHW071436160426
43195CB00013B/1925